Make a Zine!

Start Your Own Underground Publishing Revolution

Joe Biel

with Bill Brent

Microcosm Publishing

Portland, OR

Make a Zine! Start Your Own Underground Publishing Revolution
Editing © Joe Biel, 2008, 2017
This edition © Microcosm Publishing, 2008, 2017

First Edition of 5,000 copies published 1997 by Black Books
Reprint of 5,000, Oct 14, 1998
Reprint of 5,000, Jan 22, 2003
Second edition of 5,000, Dec 1, 2008
Third edition of 5,000, October 10, 2017

For a catalog, write or visit:
Microcosm Publishing
2752 N Williams Ave
Portland, OR 97227

MicrocosmPublishing.com

Isbn 978-1-62106-733-7
This is Microcosm #68

Cover designed by Joe Biel, illustrated by Matt Gauck
Edited by Sidnee Grubb & Elly Blue
Designed by Joe Biel

Distributed in the booktrade by Legato / Perseus Books Group and in the UK by Turnaround.

Microcosm Publishing is Portland's most diversified publishing house and distributor with a focus on the colorful, authentic, and empowering. Our books and zines have put your power in your hands since 1996, equipping readers to make positive changes in their lives and in the world around them. Microcosm emphasizes skill-building, showing hidden histories, and fostering creativity through challenging conventional publishing wisdom with books and bookettes about DIY skills, food, bicycling, gender, self-care, and social justice. What was once a distro and record label was started by Joe Biel in his bedroom and has become among the oldest independent publishing houses in Portland, OR. We are a politically moderate, centrist publisher in a world that has inched to the right for the past 80 years.

Global labor conditions are bad, and our roots in industrial Cleveland in the 70s and 80s made us appreciate the need to treat workers right. Therefore, our books are MADE IN THE USA and printed on post-consumer paper.

Dedicated to zine and sexuality pioneer

Bill Brent

1960-2012

Bill conceived of the idea for this book in 1997 and wrote the majority of the first edition.

He famously taught the world:

"Passion will get you through times of no technique better than technique will get you through times of no passion."

5% of the profits from this book will be donated on his behalf to the San Francisco Center for Sex and Culture

illustrations

Matt Gauck drew the illustrations on the cover and page 25. He makes the zine *Next Stop Adventure*.

Sparky Taylor drew the octopus on page 20, as well as numerous other illustrations of markers, scissors, giraffes, and zinesters on pages 12, 23, 24, 39, 40, 59, 68, 70, 101, 108, 133, 134, 147, and 156. She encouraged me to work on this book and helped to create a great vision for the 2008 edition.

David Dean is a funny and swell man who teaches in Tulsa, Oklahoma by day and draws charming bears by night like those on pages 8-10, 13-15, 61, 118, and 154.

Nate Powell has a very strict breakfast routine and is the *New York Times* bestselling author of *March*. He did the illustrations on pages 52 and 79.

Alec Longstreth has inspired many of my friends to draw comics and he works like Stephen King, 9-5 daily. He did the drawering on page 103 and does a comic called *Phase 7*.

Mike Taylor gave me the best walking tour of Providence, RI. He makes zines like *Scenery* and *Late Era Clash* and drew the picture on page 107.

Ethan Clarke has a single argyle sock tattoo. His zine, *Chihuahua and Pitbull*, is hilarious as are his books *Chainbreaker Bike Book* and *Leaning With Intent to Fall*. He did the picture on page 119.

Erin Tobey reads more fantasy and science fiction books than anything else. She makes the zine *Here It Is* and did the illustration on page 132.

Bill Brown is perhaps the friendliest person I have ever met. He lives somewhere new everytime I talk to him. He does the zine *Dream Whip* and drew the illo on page 99, and 110.

John Meijas got a second job as a baker to keep the price of his zine down. What's cooler than that? He does the zine *Paping* and did the picture on page 76.

Ben Snakepit told me that he was DIY because he catches his own fish. He does the zine *Snake Pit* and drew the illustration on page 59.

Keith Rosson is a grumpy old man with a heart of gold. Just ignore the surly exterior and bitterness that 25 years of publishing his zine *Avow* doesn't help him to sell his novel. He illustrated page 143.

Steve Larder makes the zine *Rum Lad* and did the cryptic illustration on page 145.

Julia Wertz once came to me to settle a bet. She is an illustrator for *The New Yorker,* made the zine *Fart Party,* and still works with tiny presses to publish her books. She drew page 151.

Fly has been extremely supportive of my work since I met her. She has genuine youthful excitement and energy and does the zine *Peops* and *Dog Dayz*. She wrote the comix chapter and page 64 illo.

Andy Singer draws complex ideas into simple cartoons in his zine and syndicated news strip, *No Exit*. He drew page 72.

Nate Beaty used to host mix-tape making parties where everyone contributed a song who attended. He programs on a computer all day so he drew one on page 114. He makes a zine and book called *Brainfag*.

Shawn Granton loves burritos, riding his bike, and talking about history. I mean, lots of people do, but not like this guy. He writes *Ten Foot Rule* and *Zinester's Guide to Portland* and drew page 155.

Clyde Peterson makes spacey music videos, manages the band Earth, and makes the zine *In My Room*. He drew 105.

Ramsey Beyer writes a zine called *List* so she drew the Appendices page on 159.

Ashley Rowe Palafax is a vegan that is very particular about her vegetables. We once tried to figure out how to outsmart a TV show trying to profile her. She makes *Barefoot in the Kitchen* and drew page 6.

Greig Means is a thoughtful librarian and basketball lover. He made the zine *Clutch* and did the llustration on page 30.

Eleanor Whitney is on the same "every four years" publishing schedule for her zine, *Indulgence*, that I am. Her intelligence and analytical skills give me hope in humanity's future. She drew page 124.

Adam Gnade is a songwriter, former newspaper editor, superstar, and most importantly has believed in my work and future when I didn't. He drew page 21, 22, 29, 34, 58, 60, 63, 70, 71, 75, 106.

Pete Glanting is one of the most promising new wave of cartoonists. He drew pages 141-142

contents

Foreword to the 20th Anniversary Edition

Azine is a love letter about the author's obsessions, despite its obfuscated word origin in the 1920s. Zines have more in common with books than magazines and can be as off-the-cuff as they can be bereft of highfalutin ideas. A zine showcases the subject that you just can't stop thinking about. The editor's enthusiasm and unique worldview is so genuine and infectious that readers become hooked on topics that that they didn't know they were interested in.

A zine offers a window into someone else's fascinations without the clinical or academic distance that often comes in books or newspapers. While zines were originally ways for fans to elaborate on their science fiction and wrestling fandom, they were later embraced by DIY subcultures such as the beat poets, punk rock, and street art.

Zines are beautifully unique creatures like dinosaurs or unicorns, only limited by our imaginations. They are a product of lived experiences and culture without the limitations of having to compete in a commercial marketplace. If someone tried to copy someone else's form or style, they simply couldn't make something as interesting or with the same level of authenticity. Each zine comes uniquely from the person whose mind created it. Everything is distinct in its viewpoint, from *Quitter Quarterly* to *Brown People for Black Power* to *Motorbooty,* a zine about population control...for bands!

Over the past twenty years I have been asked hundreds of times "Why are zines still relevant? Wouldn't it be much easier just to post your writing on the Internet?" "It would be easier to sit at home in my underwear and drink beer" said Aaron Cometbus, publisher of the most prolific zine of all time, *Cometbus*, in a 2000 interview with Larry Livermore. Making a zine was *never* about doing what was easiest. Today, the website Etsy features 3,000-50,000 zines for sale at any given time and there's plenty more zine writers that would never be caught dead with their blood, sweat, and tears for sale on that website. Publishing a zine is about relating to a person's experience in a safe and respectful environment where they are free to honestly exchange ideas with their peers. Nearly 100 years after it began, it remains a subculture within a sea of other subcultures.

In 2011, *Time* magazine reported about highbrow magazine creatives congregating in a ritzy New York City bar for a zine release party. Their zines reflected their passions divorced from a world of deadlines and doldrums. *Time* cited a 20-year peak in zine publishing activity. When staff writer Meredith Melnick asked the creatives "Why," *Vanity Fair*'s digital design editor Hamish Robertson spelled it out that "I'm the biggest fan of print in the boundaries that it creates, especially because my day job is working on the web. Too many people think that you can just let the page get longer and longer on a website, and while that's true, it doesn't always make it better." Katie Haegele of *White Elephants* has explained, "There's a pleasure in making it difficult for yourself. Other people appreciate it and it appeals to them when you explain, 'I sewed this together.'" Claire Heslop, creator of *The Sun Shines on it Twice*, quit blogging to return to zinemaking, explaining to the *Winnipeg Free Press,* "[Blogging] didn't really work for me, I didn't get any enjoyment out of it, it didn't feel satisfying. It's not the same as having a real, small, colourful and crazy interactive piece of something that somebody made by hand for you."

In an interview with ABC News in Melbourne, Australia, Thomas

Blatchford, a volunteer at zine store Sticky Institute, explained this motivation further. Contrary to what skeptics have convinced themselves of, according to Blatchford, zines have "definitely become much more popular recently" in part because "There's some horrible people on [the Internet.]"

I too have noticed how behavior on the Internet can be quite "horrible" so I sought out to understand why. Reading on the Internet triggers very harsh reactions in our amygdala. The amygdala is the part of the brain with the neurons that yank our control away from our thinking brain and tell us that we are under attack. The amygdala anonymously writes reactive comments all over the Internet without consequence that range from intolerant and uninformed to downright cruel and abusive. This is why zines are a safe place to exchange ideas. Dr. Faith Harper, creator of the zine *5 Minute Therapy,* who holds a PhD in counselor education and supervision, says "Like handwriting instead of typing, anything that slows down our communication process is inherently more reflexive."

Zines, like all tactile paper reading, tap into the deepest part of the brain where we retain the information that we read, according to a 2014 study reported in *The Guardian*[1]. Or as *Scientific American* puts it, unlike reading on paper, reading on the Internet "prevents people

1 TheGuardian.com/books/2014/aug/19/readers-absorb-less-kindles-paper-study-plot-ereader-digitisation

from navigating long texts in an intuitive and satisfying way"[2] because it doesn't signal the correct neurons in their brain. So we learn and remember more when we read zines too.

When I was diagnosed with Asperger's Syndrome, an autism spectrum disorder, I knew that I had to write a zine about the revelations and experiences. Indeed, people had written terrible comments in response when I wrote about my experiences on the Internet, from denying my diagnosis to telling me to kill myself. I knew that writing a zine about it would draw out my Aspie peers and future friends. It would create the community that was lacking in my immediate life and even on the Internet. And it has, beyond my wildest expectations. I was able to compare symptoms and struggles with people all over the globe and talk about how Asperger's impacted our relationships and just wasn't understood by the people that we loved. In those moments, I felt less lonely. I felt like I was a part of something.

When I made a zine about getting a vasectomy in 2003, I was able to share the experience with plenty of individuals who were peripherally interested; many even wrote to tell me about their own vasectomy experiences. When I created a zine about the Puerto Rican Independence Movement, I received numerous responses from former

---

2 Scientificamerican.com/article/reading-paper-screens/

movement members and admirers alike, as well as those who were not that familiar with the topic or had no idea that the leader was recently assassinated by the FBI.

If someone takes the time to respond to something that you've written in a zine, it's done out of love, respect, and the desire for a connection, even if it's constructive criticism. Pam Mueller, a Princeton researcher, demonstrated that people actually learn more and are more thoughtful when they write letters by hand because they synthesize their thoughts instead of just repeating information. Or as Blatchford puts it "People like to know that when they're sharing something, there are often going to be like-minded people reading...people feel a sense of trust within the zine community." Zines are a place where ideas can be nurtured as they develop. As Gillian Beck says in a 2003 interview in the documentary film *$100 and a T-shirt,* "Zines are one of the only mediums where people care enough to give feedback and criticize your work" and it's because we are all part of the same community, with similar goals.

The technicalities of zine-making take a back seat to what you're trying to express, whether it's something that you need to purge from yourself by writing, or creating art that you don't have another outlet for, or information that you feel needs to be broadcast. Or as Megulon-5, editor of *Chunk 666,* says "The kind of people that have something to say will find zines and figure out how to make them, even if it's by taking one apart and reinventing it."

Introduction

When I was fifteen years old in 1992, I went to see some underground bands that I liked perform at The Euclid Tavern in Cleveland, a bar that was neck deep in the history of rock and roll. At least the cigarette smoke was polite enough to conceal the more sinister odors lingering below the surface. Unbeknownst to me, the booking agent was flyer illustrator (now world famous tour promoter, gallery artist, and clothing mogul) Derek Hess, who booked the bands solely out of personal interest between chopping chicken wings in the kitchen. An hour after the listed start time, the bands were still nowhere to be seen so my friends and I began to lounge at the bar in wait.

Before long, a well-dressed man with sunglasses wandered up, looking a little too excited about life. He thrust an oversized, glossy magazine at me and shouted over the house music "It's by the editors of *Raygun,* that really cool zine. You know it?" I shook my head. I didn't know what a zine was for that matter. I shooed him away. His style didn't jive with me or with Cleveland. He seemed disingenuous.

Apparently looking like the easy marks that we were, a man with messy blonde hair wearing a thrift-store t-shirt and bent glasses wandered up. "Wanna buy my zine?" he asked as if he didn't care either way. I casually took it from his hands, thumbing through it.

"What's it about?" I asked him, somewhat reluctantly. He became a little more engaged.

"It's got stuff about mullets, late-night bike rides, a comic about a carnivore fighting a cannibal, bands that I like, the history of AC/DC...shit like that. It's a buck." He responded, looking me in the eye now. I handed him a buck and he let me keep the copy I was holding. The title was *Summer* and the cover was adorned with a schizophrenic collage pasted and xeroxed in a manner that was aesthetically unlike anything that I'd ever seen.

Seconds later, yet another kid walked up. He was about my age,

very short, had a huge afro, and a bigger smile. He had the enthusiasm of a carnival barker and an even simpler pitch "Zine for a quarter?" After shelling out a whole dollar a minute prior, it was a deal. His zine was called *Beckett Tapes*.

The next day at school my friends and I obsessed over those two zines. They were clever, obnoxious, and sacrilegious. I read them each two or three times that day and talked about all of the articles with my friends. It became apparent that even in a sea of boredom and sterile literature, interesting things could still somehow exist and squeeze their way into the mix. It turned on a light in the dark recesses of my brain. The existence of these zines opened me up to just how vivid the myriad of possibilities in life were. Soon thereafter, I co-founded an underground newspaper in my high school but my creative input into the education environment was not appreciated. The paper was summarily banned and any student caught with a copy was suspended. Still, *Summer* and *Beckett Tapes* remained major influences in my life. That same year I was publishing my own zine. Within three more years, I founded a publishing company that I still own and manage independently over twenty years later. I don't remember anything about the bands at the Euclid Tavern on that fated night but I still have those first zines.

The editors were Beckett Warren and Jake Kelly. I paid attention to both of them as they evolved and matured. Jake is now a rugged painter, illustrator, and artist with more interesting  things to say than most most people whose work is included in galleries. Beckett owns a gaming store in Cleveland and seems to have more political degrees and disagreeable opinions than most people I know. He was once arrested for shouting from his apartment balcony to a stranger below how excited he was about the mesh shorts that he was wearing. The stranger thought that he was a flasher and called the police.

Unbeknownst and irrelevant to me, zines were all the rage in the mainstream at the time. They were getting written up in the hip teen mag *Sassy*, acknowledged on MTV, and talked about in advertising as a vital cultural touchstone of what was cool. Before long, major publishers even tried to package and produce some awkward books about zines that flopped miscrably. But in my universe, virtual light years away from New York City, this experience taught me that you don't need to ask or receive permission to express your honest self. You can find the other weirdos simply by twisting yourself into the a fetal position on the floor and desperately yelling into the void.

Close your eyes and think for a minute. Think about something that you are passionate about and have opinions that you'd like to express. Maybe you don't like how other people are writing about a certain subject or they are neglecting what is most interesting or important about it to you. That's what your zine is about! Ayun Halliday, who keeps a public diary of her growing children and life as an artist in the zine *East Village Inky* told me  that her zine is "a long-running labor or love, in which the lack of an editor allows me to indulge my love of run on sentences that go for more than a page." Passion gets you through times of no technique better than technique gets you through times of no passion. Readers know and respond to the difference. Stick to your passions and thrive.

Zines have harbored such esoteric obsessions as the history of collectible shoes, an encyclopedia of items purchased from thrift stores, instructions for self care, a diary of washing dishes in all 50 states, punk anthropology, Springsteen fandom, news clippings of cats hating cops, submitting one's body to medical studies, stories of growing up as a Black punk, gross food photos, diatribes about body acceptance, secrets about sordid affairs, diaries of sneaking around abandoned buildings, critiques of anarchist theory, and unsent letters to people that have harmed the author. Zines can contain anything: comics, fiction, poetry, recipes, crafting instructions, artwork that can be interpreted differently by each reader, music reviews, or diary rants.

Creating zines is a way of publishing that avoids the problems of working in an increasingly stringent and impenetrable mainstream. Zines can express minority opinions, and offer space for those who aren't professional writers or artists to write and produce art. They can provide space for people to learn to refine their skills or work out their ideas. They can be anonymous. Instead of producing work for a mainstream or undetermined audience, zinesters produce work for their own ever-growing community.

Vikki Law explains why she makes a zine about women in prison, called *Tenacious*: "In the zine community, people will read a zine about issues like the problems of women in prisons, that normally would not appear on their radar or be encountered in other media."

No one needs to approve your ideas as "good enough." The very fact that they are your ideas make them worthy of sharing with your peers. If you're wondering whether this results in a glut of unreadable zines, well, there's a few. And still, they remain an important form of self-expression for their creators. But in general, the opposite is true; especially compared to the amount of pointless dreck produced by any major press during a given year. Without gatekeepers, zines allow their creators to be as authentic, expressive, and weird as they desire. After the TV show *Star Trek* launched in 1965, an audience of 500 women began writing fanzines about Kirk and Spock, the main male characters, engaged in sexual situations with each other. They were dubbed "K/S fanzines," and made fun of by sci fi and *Star Trek* fans alike, but they traded within their network, reclaiming the means of erotic production.

Zines have existed in virtually every imaginable format, from a letter in an envelope to a paperback book to an elaborate construction where every page has some sort of compartment to open, each containing more interactive parts and three-dimensional fold-outs.

Most zines are written, designed, and constructed by one person with a print run of a few hundred copies but that doesn't mean that yours has to be. "*Plumplandia*'s mission is to spread fat positivity and body love by sharing the works created by Portland's amazing fat community!" says its co-editor, Leathia Miller. As Rebecca Gilbert explains in *$100 & A T-Shirt,* the determining factor of whether a publication is a zine or not is based on the principal motivation of its creator. "The intention to foster some kind of community; to educate; to have fun; those all are part of what a zine is."

Zinesters often are the first to capture changes in culture because their authors are closer to the action than their ivory-tower counterparts. Music zines usually cover bands that will never break commercially and are more interesting than those "discovered" by music magazines. Zines contain some of the most unique and subversive writing and thought available.

In practice, most zines have more in common with art objects than magazines; for instance, hand-made on specialty paper or brown grocery bags, bound with twine, hand or machine sewn bindings, fastened with metal brads, rubber bands or duct tape, adorned with stickers, glitter, photographs, or rubber stamps, and covers lovingly silkscreened by hand or printed by Gocco, a japanese toy that creates a handy way to put ink onto paper at home.

Some zines are typeset and printed by hand entirely on a letterpress machine. Each issue is an original, limited edition piece of art. These zine makers have reclaimed the means of production—in every way—writing, designing, printing, distributing, and financing.

Because we produce our work outside of the mainstream, zinesters use alternative distribution channels as well. Zines are distributed through top-secret bedroom distributors and sent through the mail in decorated envelopes to stores located in alley basements. Websites like Facebook, Twitter, and Etsy allow zinesters to promote their work and find other people's creations. A few prodigious people even created ZineWiki.com, an open-source online encyclopedia of zines, and WeMakeZines.com, a social networking site for zinemakers.

People who make and read zines don't fit easily into demographic groups. They include college students, teachers, home-schoolers, wingnuts with library cards, radical moms, transgender people, librarians, cartoonists, comedians, activists, organic farmers, childhood abuse survivors, dumpster divers and squatters, disillusioned middle-class working people, award-winning writers, bored teenagers, sex workers, and anyone who has ever found themselves on the fringes of society or literature. But what's best is that these people aren't only interested in zines about their own hobbies and experiences. They are interested in zines about subjects that they didn't even know they were interested in yet, including yours! Perhaps zines are the warm hug in the cold world that you've been waiting for! Let's go!

8 Steps to Making a Zine.

After endlessly rereading *Summer* and *Beckett Tapes*, over the next few weeks, eventually I pulled out the staples and tried to figure out how to make my own. It was a completly logical next step. Everything about the zines screamed "You can do this! Look how easy it is!" Within a few months I had printed my first issue of *Stink in Public*.

Step One. Write something! It doesn't matter whether you handwrite your words, type them, or cut-and-paste in ransom note style. Virtually anything is acceptable and that is the beauty of zines.

Zine aesthetics vary widely in style, professionalism, and quality. Go to your local library and spend an afternoon browsing books on graphic design. Order some zines through the mail and look at photos of them online. Read a few dozen zines and figure out what you like and don't like. If you like someone's ideas, be inspired to creatively respond to them in your own zine. This can help develop a sense of your own aesthetic preferences for graphic style. A lot of zinesters skip developing their own graphic style or refine it gradually over time, but it's worth spending time thinking about. You're making a piece of art and even this aspect should contain a small piece of yourself.

Step Two. Find some pictures to go with your words. They can be photos, collages, line art, drawings, or anything else you can dream up. Do the best job you can to reproduce your images. (Images snagged from the Web are probably not of high enough resolution to reproduce well on paper...but if you distort and edit them enough, they create their own appealing look!). Some zines use very few images, which can make it more difficult to hold your attention. Using images to break up the repetitiousness of words on the page will help readers enjoy your zine and express a greater number of ideas at once.

> ACTION ITEM! Far more people will pick up a zine with an interesting or provocative cover. If you're planning to sell your zine, visit a place that sells zines and notice which ones grab your attention. Try to figure out why.

Step Three. Set your price. Usually this is free to $10. You may want to base your price on the cost of copying, including paper, stapling, and folding, postage, and perhaps something for your time (even if it's just coffee, cookies, or

the occasional slice of pizza!). If there are other expenses (PO Box rental, envelopes, stamps for letters, etc.), plan for those as well. Most people who will sell your zine for you, like stores and distributors, will take 40-60% of the cover price. If you want to sell your zine through these channels, think about this when setting your price. You can just have a direct relationship with your readers through the mail if you prefer.

Step Four. Include your address. This is vital. Many people include both a postal address and an e-mail address. The best place is the back cover or first page. Of course, if you're publishing something subversive or illegal you may not want it traced back to you. It is easy to be anonymous with the way that zine distribution functions. You may feel more comfortable renting a PO Box for security and privacy than printing your home address. You can rent a box from the Postal Service (cheapest) or from a private mail drop company (twice as much). A private mail drop may be more convenient if they have longer hours and can accept a wider range of deliveries. Some provide copying services and other conveniences. One zinester told me that he rents a private mailbox because its address resembles an apartment's. It has tricked would-be stalkers and creeps into trying to visit. Be safe!

Steve Kudlak, West Virginia Zine Archivist, also points out that "PO Boxes provide a stable address for people who move frequently and don't get along with their previous landlords."

Step Five. Print some copies. Unless you're blessed with deep pockets or unlimited access to free copies, it's a safe bet to make 30-200 photocopies to start. If you are making drastically fewer, laser printing at home may make more sense. If you are making 1,000+, it may make sense to work with an offset printer. If you want it to look like a book, you can hire a digital printer like Lightning Source.

Unless you have an obvious place to make copies (read: "free"), it makes sense to call around and figure out who has the best price for what you are printing. Sometimes one shop will match or beat another's price. Don't be afraid to ask for a deal, but it is more likely in smaller copy shops than national chains—though sometimes an individual staff person will take a liking to your project and help you out! Befriending the staff will also make your relations much more pleasant.

It's helpful to ask people who do zines where they print them, especially if you like the production values of their zine or you have a hunch that they have the hookup somewhere. Respect the printer—especially if it's an employee doing a "favor" for you. A good shop is an invaluable source of information on how to adjust the size of your zine, page count, or colors to get the lowest price. The more controversial your material is, the more important it is to have a strong, personal relationship with your printer. There are many horror stories of trying to get sexually-oriented material, anti-Republican propaganda, or even zines with peculiar names printed. Stewart Anderson, editor of the facetiously named *Midget Breakdancing Digest,* says that he was hung up on by more printers than he worked with. On the other hand, there is no reason to work with someone who is disrespectful to you or your work.

Step Six. Get reviewed! Send copies of your zine to publications like *Xerography Debt* and the others here.[3] It's a simple and effective way to find people interested in reading your zine and communicating with people who share your interests. Because that's what it's all about, right?

Step Seven. Distribute your zine. Think about who to give or sell your zine to. It could be friends, family, co-workers, Facebook groups with similar interests, or other people who make zines. These people can be reached through reviews, local stores, far away stores, social media, and distributors ("distros").[4]

Step Eight. A mailing list. Figure out a way to keep track of who you are in touch with and who is interested in your work. You can keep track of them with scraps of paper in a shoebox, an Excel spreadsheet, a notebook, a computer database, a card file, or an address book in an email program, as long as you can find the information when you need it.

Making a zine is that simple. Everything else is based on these eight basic steps.

3 https://brooklyncollegezines.commons.gc.cuny.edu/zine-resources/
4 http://zinewiki.com/List_of_Distros

Why Make a Zine?

When I started making my own zine, I made a huge mistake early on: I created a completely arbitrary production schedule. I planned to make a new issue every two months, which created a cascading set of deadlines. This restriction sucked almost all of the fun and life out of the zine. It came to feel like another responsibility amid my busy-yet-aimless teenage life. I didn't figure out the most important aspect of making a zine until I was in my twenties: work on it when the muse strikes and ignore it when it doesn't. And in the years since then I've learned that taking the pressure off makes it not only more fun, but I actually get more done. Even if that means that sometimes take a break for four years before coming back to it.

Sometimes the best motivation is to read great zines about other people's passions. John Marr explores bizarre cases of death in each issue of *Murder Can Be Fun*. Eric Ruin, Meredith Stern, and Andy Cornell use their zines, *Trouble in Mind, Crude Noise*, and *Secret Files of Captain Sissy* to dissect, critique, and discuss the radical political movements that they are a part of. Lauren Martin wrote intellectual feminist and cultural critique in her zine, *Quantify*. Dave Roche wrote *On Subbing* to tell his daily stories of working as a substitute special education assistant in Portland's public schools. *Shark Fear, Shark Awareness* is exactly what the name suggests: An informative and reverent guide to sharks!

You may want to create a zine to have your work in print or to share what you make. To encourage others creatively. To explore subjects that fascinate you. To connect with folks who share your interests. To get mail. To make new friends. To create the kind of publication you've always wished existed. To communicate very passionately in a medium that is intensely personal. Whatever your interests or agendas, a zine allows you to express your opinions, art, and ideology to an audience in a fun, cheap, meaningful way.

For still others, making a zine helps to deal with living in an insane world. On the newsgroup alt.zines, Christine, author of *Post Modern Toad*, posted:

> "Doing something creative is therapeutic. For me, the creative urge has always seemed to scream during the most difficult times in my life. I've learned to *never* ignore that urge when I'm feeling down—unexpressed creative energy

makes me feel even worse! Who needs that? Focusing that energy on doing something positive is a hell of a lot more constructive than sitting around feeling sorry for yourself. If someone doesn't understand it, or doesn't appreciate it, or even if they totally hate it...that really doesn't matter at all. Before anyone else has even seen it, it's served its purpose—you've accomplished something to be proud of. If you've entertained someone else in the process, all the *more* power to you!"

"The most important zine you will ever make is your first zine. It is likely to be awful and that is okay, even encouraged. Zines are always works in progress, just like people." offers Davida Breier, editor of *Xerography Debt*. Your first zine is a learning process. You make it, get feedback, learn from your mistakes, and keep getting better. If you saw the early issues of some long-running zines, you'd be shocked at how rough they were. Better to get it done than to delay by trying to make it perfect. Once you get over your fear and get that first issue in people's hands, you'll find the second one is a lot easier. Either you'll want to prove to folks it wasn't a fluke, or you'll want to show them you're capable of even better.

"I was heartbroken recently when a new trade partner said that he felt bad for sending me such 'shit' after he saw my zines. I don't see any quality difference in what he does and what I do. What I do see is someone who gets down on himself and what he creates—and other people like him." Jaime Nyx of the review website SeaGreenZines.com told me.

In five years, you might have different thoughts and opinions; better skills at design. You'll cringe at the awful layout and groan as you read the awkward phrasing. You won't be alone but it was an honest snapshot of your expression at that time.

Most great zines are great because the editor felt driven to publish them. A great zine transcends limitations of funds, likelihood, experience, and technology. The vast majority of zines don't make it to issue five. It's hard to sustain the enthusiasm that got the creators started. Family commitments, work, loss of interest, and plain old burnout get in the way, and the zine is abandoned, often leaving a trail of disappointed fans in its wake.

But zines are fun while they last, both for the writer and the reader. And the definitions of "writer" and "reader" can be amazingly fluid. This is one of the most exciting things about zines. Many readers of a zine eventually became its writers, and many readers are inspired to produce their own zines. As Clem Burke, who has drummed for Blondie and the Ramones, once said, "The ultimate fan transcends fandom and does it themselves."

Still, there's not much point in blatantly copying someone else's zine. You want to learn from others' mistakes and successes, not steal them. Revisit your own motivations periodically so that the project stays within your vision and so your initial motivations remain.

Start an issue with one of your strongest pieces to get people's attention right away. Don't start the issue with something that is more than a few pages long. Inserting graphics early on helps, since this also gets readers into the zine more quickly. Think about what you want to say, how you want to say it, how you want it to flow, what order it will appear in, and where that material will come from. And watch it evolve.

Madeleine Baran, former editor of *Tight Pants* and now an investigative reporter who spends weeks digging up facts for American Public Media, joked that, "People say that it takes months to write a zine but I would just stay up all night in one giant candy-and-caffeine-fueled binge and write the whole thing at once." And she's right. Some people meticulously spend months proofreading every article while others write a one-draft zine with nothing more than a pen or clunk it out on a manual typewriter. Beginners tend to type their zine on a computer, print it out, and paste it onto the page with a gluestick over graphics. Experiment and think about what would be most comfortable for you as well as

the best form to express what you have to say.

This project is all up to you. You are the writer, artist, publisher, and distributor, so it's all about creating something that you care about and that is true to your vision. Finding and developing that vision is one of the simplest tenets of making a zine.

While I continued to devour every zine that entered my path throughout the nineties, I did not give any thought or interest to where this movement came from or why. Deep in the back of my mind, I assumed that it had always been fueled by disillusioned teens like myself. And this assumption was surprisingly accurate. Granted, 25 years later I realize the value of recognizing that you are part of something, learning from the past, and making informed decisions based on what has and has not worked historically.

Much conjecture has been thrown around that publications like Thomas Paine's *Common Sense* in 1775 was an early zine. Its radical point of view changed public opinion and ultimately led to the colonies taking up insurrectionary arms, causing the United States to become an independent global superpower. Your zine may or may not have such lasting impacts but it doesn't mean that you shouldn't try.

Around the same time, there was Benjamin Franklin's zine *Poor Richard's Almanac.* Consisting of poetry and articles about health, disease, and medicine written by Franklin and distributed to patients and hospital staff, the zine came to be influential in shaping medical thoughts and theories, while entertaining those in need of a laugh. Starting in 1732 and publishing until 1759, Franklin's zine came to be quite influential to the medical community, not only due to his skills behind the pen, but also because he was as opinionated as he was definitive. His motivations remain remarkably similar to contemporary zinemakers and he convinced us to stop trying to treat paralysis with electroshock therapy.

Not all zinemakers were white guys with wigs, though much less has been said about the zines going back to 1440 that shared information about witchcraft and demonology for women healers. These zines became especially important as a way to learn and communicate after witchhunts began in Europe.

With the introduction of the printing press in 1454, moveable metal type and ink made from turpentine, lampblack, and linseed oil allowed mass production for the first time. Within 50 years, over 500,000 texts had been printed. Almost all of them were religious works, so naturally the number of zines about exposing the dangers of witchcraft and identifying witches quickly outnumbered zines by witches. Throughout Europe, because of the printing press, the inquisition distributed a uniform procedure for persecuting witches in *Malleus Malefactorum.* As the church's concern about witches has lessened in recent years, modern teenagers have seen to returning the numbers in favor of zines for witches.

Just like modern teenagers, Martin Luther began attacking the Vatican with his zine, which he would literally nail to church doors. Just like Thomas Paine, his zine started a war.

Starting in the 1840s, the women's suffrage movement created their own brand of trouble by publishing zines within their community. Run by affluent white women who were forbidden from working, the suffrage movement was comprised of prolific zine makers. Matilda Joslyn Gage, editor of *The National Citizen*, was so radical in her zine's suffragist and abolitionist proclamations—incorporating the rights of Native Americans, the church's role in subjugating women, prison rights, and motions towards racial justice—that her relatively conservative peers wrote her out of history. Fortunately, her zines live on.

But it wasn't until 1929 that we began calling them zines...well, fanzines. During the Great Depression, readers of science fiction pulps became increasingly frustrated with inaccuracies and poor writing. They wrote angry letters to the editor criticizing the quality of the stories, nitpicking technical details about science and the temperature of the sun, etc. Frustrated, the pulp editors responded by printing the critics' full addresses. The critics responded by writing to each other and sending their own homemade fan-magazines—fanzines—to each other.

Before long, the first global fanzine networks were created through the postal system. Within a few years there was a loose network of fanzines about topics such as horror, wrestling, and science fiction. *The Comet,* a science fiction zine composed mostly of articles on science, began publishing in 1930. Other science fiction zines followed, including *Time Traveler* and *Science Fiction,* edited by Jerome Siegel and Joe Schuster, who became the creators of Superman. Horror author H. P. Lovecraft developed a major crush on the self-publishing movement.

A high schooler named Chester Carlson, who had been self-publishing his work since 1924 with the help of the mimeograph, took the movement one step further in 1938 when he obtained the patents for his new invention, the photocopier. Carlson had invented "dry copy" that he called Xerography, based on the Greek word for "dry writing."

In 1944 the Battle Development Company began producing the first xerox machine and became the Xerox Corporation. The first commercial photocopier was introduced in 1958 and self-publishing soared.

Immediately, underground cartoonists began publishing via xerox as did household names like *Rolling Stone,* which started as a zine in 1967 with Hunter S. Thompson's political reporting. In The Soviet Union, self-publishers risked their lives by sharing their thoughts and opinions with each other. Tatyana M. Velikanova, one of three publishers of *The Chronicle of Current Events,* spent four years in a prison camp and five years in exile for printing her views.

The 1950s saw the Beats discovering the mimograph and self-publishing their first writings. While nothing like the Soviets, Americans in the 1960s faced lesser persecution for publishing their work, such as Alan Ginsberg's poem *Howl*. Ginsberg was subjected to a long court trial in which poets and professors were summoned to "prove" that *Howl* was not obscene.

In 1975, seemingly in response to the men who had been elbowing women out of publishing scenes for hundreds of years, Janice Bogstad created *Janus,* a feminist sci-fi zine that featured writers including Octavia Butler and Joanna Russ. Bogstad brought a feminist edge to science fiction and cultivated a generation of women sci-fi authors that thrived in its community. The zine was nominated for a Hugo Award in 1978, 1979, and 1980 and was subsequently taken over by an editorial committee who changed the name to *Aurora*. The committee published until 1990 when their energy and attention were fully committed to WisCon, the leading feminist science fiction convention that continues to this day.

Simultaneously in New York City, in a parallel world to the Beats, sci-fi fans, and West Coast hippie comix artists, was a teenager named John Holmstrom. Holmstrom was a student at the School of Visual Arts who approached the dean and demanded a cartooning program. After his demand was met and world-famous cartoonists Harvey Kurtzman and Will Eisner were hired, Holmstrom dropped out and began working for Kurtzman and Eisner. Next,

Holmstrom did what any respectable twenty-something would: in 1975 he created a national zine about the infant music movement that he and his friends were involved with.

Not only did Holmstrom believe—as all young people should—that what his friends were doing was something of global significance, he literally coined the name *Punk* to describe this new music scene. The inaugural issue featured an impulsive cover feature about the Ramones and a hilarious interview with Lou Reed, who happened to be in the audience on the night when the editors interviewed the Ramones. Reed reluctantly agreed to talk to the editors. According to Holmstrom, in an interview with Aaron Cometbus, it was the article in *Punk* that got the Ramones their record deal.

Punk appeared on newsstands in England and seemed to represent a social movement that was larger than life. Other American and British punks adopted the language and carried the banner, publishing zines about their local scenes throughout the late 1970s and early 1980s. Even better, Holmstrom created the bold, eye-popping aesthetic that continues to be mimicked in zines to this day, punk and otherwise. Perhaps the most famous result of *Punk* is *Maximum Rocknroll*, which has been publishing monthly for over 35 years.

And let's face it. No one is going to write about our social movements and if they do, they won't get the details right. Better to do it ourselves.

Born of similar muster to *Punk*, *Factsheet Five* was founded by Mike Gunderloy in 1982 to document sci-fi zines. Gunderloy came to find zines of all types and subjects fascinating and *Factsheet Five* eventually focused on zines as their own subculture scene. He popularized shortening fanzine to "zine" and established guidelines that a zine should be motivated around the importance of building community and feedback from readers. After ten years of being the publisher, Gunderloy sold the rights to other editors before *Factsheet Five* folded for good in 1998.

Throughout the 1980s, zines became the megaphone for anyone to express their political, artistic, and social views and experiences. *Juvenile Delinquents* (*J.D.s*) was created because the editors, GB Jones and Bruce LaBruce, felt that as punk turned into crossover metal it had lost its sexual diversity and traded in its oddball values for mainstream macho ones.

In 1989 Jones and LaBruce wrote a satirical editorial in *Maximum Rocknroll* titled "Don't Be Gay," about punk's replication of traditional values that made it so white, male, straight, and gender binary. The article resulted in a flood of mail from people that related with their experience and perspective. Soon, zines became a safe place for queers to build community and a social movement too. The resulting homocore zine explosion is still felt to this day.

In 1985, the arrival of digital typesetting made it much easier to make a zine but zinesters continued to clutch their typewriters and pens tightly, partly as a way to maintain a certain aesthetic and, again, partly as a way not to make this labor of love feel too much like school or work.

In the 90s, zinesters continued to ruminate about their passions and the scene gradually blossomed into a comfortable place to express any kind of personal writing or expression of issues that the editors were grappling with, from sexual assault to vegan recipes to gender identity to size acceptance to mental health to childhood abuse. Zines developed their own voice and subculture. A zine was a passageway into new, unexplored worlds and understanding experiences that were foreign from our own. It was also a warm, welcoming hug, telling us that our perspectives weren't wrong even if our parents or teachers told us that they were. At the same time you could also read about the dub scene in southern Alabama or the grindcore music in the Upper Peninsula or even what Sally saw at the strip club last Friday night—things that just weren't being written about elsewhere.

In 1991 this blossomed into the Riot Grrrl movement, a radical social movement that started in the punk scenes of DC and Olympia. Riot Grrrl was inspired to spread its feminist manifesto and women's experiences through Molly Neuman and Allison Wolfe's zine of the same name. With angry feminist screeds resembling ransom notes, a giant pressure valve exploded and re-framed the basic foundation of punk. Soon, dozens of riot girl zines appeared, showing women as equals while saying "we are creative and like to have fun too." Riot Grrrl put the women on stage—literally and metaphorically—to inspire other women in the audience to feel like they belonged there too.

In 1994, Pete Jordan, editor of *Dishwasher* was summoned to appear on the *Late Show with David Letterman*. The show had developed a habit of punching down—making fun of working-class schlubs—and a zine about washing dishes in all 50 states was the perfect mark to mock. Jordan responded with his own prank by sending his friend, zinester Jess Hilliard, to pretend to be him.

David Letterman wasn't alone. Mainstream media discovered zines as a fascinating facet of alternative music. *Bust* and *Giant Robot* were started in 1993 and 1994 as low print run, photocopied zines before quickly evolving into popular magazines available at most newsstands. Zines were talked about on MTV and bandied about in magazines like *Time, Details, Sassy,* and *GQ.* The National Public Radio syndicated program *This American Life* made a habit of featuring zines and zinesters throughout its early years. Tower Records, then a national chain, sold zines in hundreds of its stores, even in the suburbs. In 1993 I read a story in *Rolling Stone* about a junkie in San Francisco who wrote a zine. The punchline was that, just like Pete Jordan, he didn't want to be discovered. I wondered how to find a copy of his zine.

Riot Grrrl demanded that its unofficial members enforce a "media blackout" after news stories consistently reduced them into an infantilized fashion movement and a dumbed down girls vs. boys politick. Riot Grrrl had become the media anyway, now with hundreds of zines publishing under its banner. Nike hired an ad agency to publish a zine about shoes and basketball. Sirius XM radio made a zine about, well, their products. It was an odd scene. Soon, everyone saw the results of Kurt Cobain courting the media for two years and then spending the next two years trying to hide from them. Fortunately, the mainstream got bored with zines before killing them too. Besides, unlike Nirvana, the mainstream never figured out how to make money from zines. So instead, they printed articles about how zines were "over" and no one was making them anymore. Pagan Kennedy went from writing a zine to writing a memoir about how she used to make a zine to becoming the innovation columnist for the *New York Times Magazine*. The shivering zine masses that remained stopped holding their breath and let out a sigh of relief.

And naturally, the underground continued to carry the torch. Aaron Cometbus, publisher of *Cometbus* since 1981, began to travel the country after his band broke up, settling in for a few months in each city. Unlike what the name would lead you to believe, *Cometbus* is a prolific narrative that puts the personal stories into punk rock with short snapshots that reveal carefully edited observances of what it would be like to exist in his various scenes. Aaron would literally go door-to-door in each of his adopted towns, convincing comic, book, record, and coffee shops to carry his zine and, by extension, all zines. Twenty years later his network still exists and influences new stores to sell zines for similar reasons.

Across the turn of the millennium, as the Internet began to mainstream blogs and popular zines like *Thrift Score, Beer Frame,* and *Answer Me!* quit publishing, the mainstream again forecasted doom and gloom but zines marched on triumphantly. Instead of being made obsolete by the Internet, zines utilized

it as a way to find readers. Zine conferences began to appear all over the world and zinesters would travel thousands of miles to attend and meet each other.

The absence of many long-running zines and the lack of mainstream attention created a fresh, open environment. The awareness of what had come before motivated many individuals to create book-art zines and other forms requiring extensive time and effort. Many zine publishers returned to printing methods like silkscreen, letterpress, linoleum cut, and also to hand-stitched bindings.

Today, people who stick to print do so because of its warm, human feel, or distinctive artistic elements. You can use printing techniques that create texture, create pull-out sections, insert envelopes, insert bags with scents, use different kinds of paper, and incorporate other elements that make your zine unique and unable to be reproduced on-screen. Similarly, zines offer an intimate connection in the kinds of information they convey, the vulnerability that the authors often provide, and the simple fact that you can read them in the park, on the bus, or on the toilet.

Now nearly 90 years old, zines have transcended five generations with no mind paid to what is said about them by people outside of their community. It's a take-it-or-leave-it narrative because zines will always be there, lurking under the surface and exposing you to groups of people that your grandparents would be horrified about...if they knew they existed.

communities

From a very young age I gave deeply of myself for the zine community. Not only sharing my stories and secrets, but putting in over one hundred hours every week reading zines and writing postcards in response, offering constructive feedback—what I liked, what I would love. Before long I moved out of my parent's house and started Microcosm, distributing zines out of a pair of tiny closets adjoining my bedroom. While my roommates were at work from nine to five, I was writing letters and sending and receiving packages of zines. The ideas I had discovered in zines had given my life meaning and purpose. I wanted to give back. I still do, but twenty years later, I have a more nuanced understanding of how to do so and better boundaries.

Trading zines remains a great way to make friends. In fact, some zines are only available through trading—be it for another zine, music, or a letter. Zines have deep roots in anti-consumerism and trading is a vital part of the history and culture." says Davida Breier, editor of *Xerography Debt,* the review zine with perzine tendencies.

Be thoughtful of your readers, like Ayun Halliday who offers of the *East Village Inky,* "I usually give people a complimentary issue and tell them to keep it on the back of their toilet tank or at the bottom of their bag, where they may rediscover it in a long line at the bank or post office." These same readers often reappear in your life years later and remember the things that you've said. It's likely that your whimsical sentiments will be more meaningful to others than to you, so be mindful of what you write.

It is common for people who spend a few years making zines to become entrenched in the community in other ways. Zine publishers become distro operators, internet forum hosts, zine librarians, and organizers of zine conferences. It's a natural extension of their love for zines.

It is in this way that the community can mentor newcomers, with resources that enable you to talk to your peers on a level playing field. It is also these resources that sustain the energy flow and finances of the zine world. When a small group of us founded the Portland Zine Symposium, none of the original group were from Portland. None of us had even lived in Portland for more than a few years. But we had all grown up with zines as a meaningful part of our lives that we wanted to share with others. We organized as volunteers and without funding. Our enthusiasm created an internationally attended event that attracted over 1,500 people in its second year.

Within six years, the last of the original group had gone on to other things and the event was put together by younger blood who, similarly to the founders, were inspired and motivated by what the zine community represented to them. It was more important that the event continued under new leadership than it was for anyone to receive credit or ownership. In the years that followed, new zine fests popped up in Austin, Minneapolis, Philadelphia, London, Houston, Los Angeles, Kansas City, Chicago, and Richmond. A few events even came to use the name "Zine Symposium." After the emotional meetings we had to pick a name, it really touched me that we had inspired others in that way.

Zines touch a special part of our heart. Claudia McBarron teaches kids six to seventeen years old to make zines and told me "The younger students literally walk around hugging their freshly published zines."

This trust and exchange of information is why it's important to only make promises that you can keep. The fact that a stranger will let you sleep on their floor is a reason to extend the same offer to others and always be as good as your word. People are trusting and even understanding when your project is slow or falls apart.

In many ways your work begins where others have left off and continues a narrative that is nearly 100 years young. Writing a zine can feel like aiming a megaphone into an echo chamber, for better and worse. There's a set of implied ethics that come along with the benefits of being a community.

If you owe people money, do your best to pay them. You can usually work out a payment schedule, if you can't afford it all at once. Just don't leave people hanging; it builds mistrust that leaves people afraid to put dollar bills in envelopes, which creates the best feeling for all of us in the end.

The vast majority of zinesters begin in their teens. Some start even younger. Because of the strong feelings of connection, zinesters can get stuck at the emotional age that they were at when they began making zines. One resulting issue is that there's a strong resistance to growth or change. Craven Rock told me in an interview, "The idea of a 'zine community' is dictating ethics. I feel limited by the context. I am a writer who happens to be perfectly happy doing a zine, besides that dilemma, anyway...the scene also likes certain things—vegan cooking, bikes, making out, polyamoury—and as long as you wrote subject matter within their field of interest you could be a part of this scene."

Through these methods, and deconstruction of corporate culture and norms, zine makers have learned to live within the margins and build our own community with these ideas—creating collective housing, learning the medicinal properties of plants, creating community centers, making films—without a budget, and pushing the envelope of what is possible through these mediums.

While zines promote thinking about the possibilities of a self-directed life, people can feel forced to fit the mold. Michael T

Perkins, editor of arts and culture zine *Section 8* told me, "In this community, you can always count all the Black artists on one hand. Whenever people see Black artists at a zine fest they assume we are promoting a racial or political agenda. They see us behind the table and they think 'oh those are the #BlackLivesMatter zinesters.'" Others are not always welcomed. Paco Taylor, creator of 70s-influnced arts and pop culture perzine *Kung Fu Grip*, laments his experience of not feeling like he was being let into the zine community that he very much wanted to be a part of, "I wasn't white, I wasn't queer, I wasn't from middle America, I wasn't a fan of Kerouac, and I didn't listen to punk...[I felt like] an outsider even amongst cultural outsiders"

Naturally, zinedom has always been a delicate balance between maintaining a point of view and set of values with making sure that everyone is invited to the party. Because if everyone at the party is white or male or able-bodied, we are limiting the perspectives that we can learn from. But yet, the vast majority of people who show up again and again are white, male, able-bodied, and of means. Craven continues, "It is unethical to make an entire medium a 'safe place' where your particular subculture won't be offended or hurt. When zines first started there was room for everybody from [anarchist who picks fights] Bob Black to [*Redneck Manifesto* author] Jim Goad. I don't care for Jim Goad myself, but I am also an adult and can decide on my own whether or not I want to read him."

Claudia McBarron also challenges the dominant view "[It's important to] listen to individuals that hold values that might not be your own." She wants zines to find "a broader appeal that goes beyond the initial science fiction and punk roots. Not every parent wants to have their child reading about someone's uterus. Not every child wants to be reading about someone's uterus."

Contemporary zine makers have, in their quest for exclusive inclusivity, recreated a guilt-ridden, homogeneous microcosm of mainstream culture. When veteran zinester, professor, and artist Kate Bingaman-Burt charged $120 for a zinemaking workshop at a Los Angeles gallery, the zine community were quick to put all of their feelings on the table. In an online forum, complaints ranged from "I was afraid she was sort of a new zine maker capitalizing, which was awkward" to "the commodification of diy culture" to "feeds into consumerist/capitalist/colonization philosophies" to "I offer workshops for whatever people want to pay" to "it implies that if you don't have that money you can't have a 'crash course' in zines."

In the conversation, there's the palpable idea that members of the community must form an opinion and the community's perception will have consequences. And indeed it did. The zinesters publicly complained about it until the gallery dropped the price to $49 and references to zines were changed to "writing, design, and illustration." But even then, commenters wondered if they could force the price down to $20. When the conversation turned into an argument about the ethics of bullying, one person responded "I don't think you understand what the term bullying means. lol as if organizations are people. LOL." This disconnect, that people within the community are easier to impact with our frustrations, shows how zinesters sometimes react in an effort to tear things down without considering the consequences instead of challenging people in real positions of power.

I saw many of these struggles from the other side of the fence. One person sent an angry letter to the Zine Symposium claiming that we were paid for organizing the event. She did not completely back off even when we explained that we were volunteers.

Sometimes even people who are otherwise mature, developed adults return to a less emotionally mature place when describing their relationship to zines. While conducting the research for this book, someone created a social media account pretending to be me, referred to my interviews as "free labor," and proceeded to dictate who they deemed racist and anonymously bully me. Becca Confidential of *Darling Disasters* warns, "You really don't want to piss people off who are in the independent media area. They'll bite your head off worse than any kind of judge or anyone." Kari Tervo of *Shards of Glass in Your Eye* explains "There are intellectual children in the zine community who appear to think in memes...I've been physically threatened for pointing out that 'no, it is not intersectional to refuse to even read zines written by white people and pre-emptively sending them fliers stating such.' Physically. Threatened."

Zines, have become a sounding board for people's thoughts and feelings. Oftentimes, it feels like people do not evaluate the results of their words on others. Our interpretations of others' actions and motives can hurt feelings and wreck relationships. Your partner or friend will not always appreciate the artistic creative non-fiction literary device that you spun around their lifestyle. When you interpret your friends, even as fictionalized characters in a story, it is normally still obvious to them and can hurt their feelings.

Oddly, it is often the same people offering both sides of an argument in a conflicted part of their identity. They want their work to be affordable but don't want to undervalue it. They want to welcome everyone into their community but don't want to include points of view that they find offensive. Some people could see and admit that it was the mindset of their zine-making ethics that sabotaged their own success and maintained self-imposed limitations. My former co-editor Bill Brent referred to people who are verbally conflicted in this way as "Hand Wringers." It's a slippery snake pit to avoid where the tendency is forever to criticize and tear down others when we desperately need to be building each other up and demonstrating positive examples.

However, just because this exclusivity and perspective exists in the scene doesn't mean that you have to just accept it and roll over. Much like Janice Bogstad and the feminists who carved their own parallel track next to sexist science fiction in 1975 or punks who reclaimed zines from beatniks and sci-fi writers in 1977, you can leave your own mark on the zine community and challenge whichever sacred cows rub you the wrong way.

And Paco did just that. His next zine, *In His Image: Bob Marley, Haile Selassie and the Second Coming of Christ*, challenges many community norms by distilling a lot of history and exploring the origins of the Rastafari faith and religious iconography. And it was a success. "Good reviews came from divergent sources, and impressive sales came from around the world." But he still felt left out. "I just liked the idea of feeling like part of the zine community that I learned about from zines ordered by the stacks."

Ken Bausert of *The Ken Chronicles* offers a solution, "Trading zines opens peoples' eyes to new and unexplored subjects and expands our understanding or appreciation of other's views." Trading allowed Paco to find his audience alongside selling on his own website and getting reviews in magazines.

Sometimes I intentionally challenged conventions. When zine distributors Fine Print and Desert Moon were going into bankruptcy as I was starting Microcosm, I decided that I would sell zines to stores even though a community-based organization like Microcosm doing so was pretty taboo. While a few people were appalled by the concept and others wondered how I could make the numbers work, the reception was almost entirely positive. Microcosm became a way for zinesters to get their work into stores across the globe. I didn't think of this as a "business opportunity," I thought of it as a positive service for zines.

More than anything, all of these strong feelings stem from the desire to protect something magical, which we can all do in our own way. And the best part is no one can take that away from you. A really simple thing that you can do is host zine-making parties with your friends, where you come together to be creative, clack away on typewriters, and share in the joy of the creative process!

There are zine editors who want to have their cake and eat it too—achieve a level of commercial success while attempting to remain true to their underground roots—or eschewing the mainstream success to which they aspire. While I don't like hypocrisy, I don't fear it, either. Explore your true motives. Be honest with yourself. If "succeeding" preoccupies your mind, it will have a negative impact on your work and you won't last long. I have witnessed financial hardships that forced decisions that editors or publishers would not have made otherwise. This is one reason why it's always better to respond with empathy than venom. It'll lead to a better place. Treat people with respect, and you will earn respect in return. Also, seek facts and use your analytical thinking skills when presented with an argument, even one that you think you agree with.

Don't make zines to fit into another cool kid club. Make zines to create your own cool kid club. Paco eventually got over being rejected, saying, "The silver lining to all of this, of course, was that the insulated nature of the established zine community challenged me to explore other avenues, which extended my reach well beyond what I'd ever thought possible."

Kari too mostly feels positive. "I would say that I am 90 percent pleased with the zine community as a whole, but when it's present, the bullshit really likes to make a big stink."

If you always consider quitting your project, your brain will *always* point out the meaning and purpose that attracted you in the first place, which provides a positive basis to make decisions around. Your stubbornness will kick in and remind you why you stay. Maybe, like me, you'll only make a zine every few years. Do what feels right to you.

Define your own destiny by answering the following questions.

1) What kind of project do you want to operate?

2) What is your ultimate goal with the project? Write it out in one sentence as your mission statement.

3) What kind of legal structure do you want to have, if any? Will there ever be efforts to provide wages or stipends?

4) What kind of time commitment do you have to commit to the project?

5) Will other people help you? Will you be able to relinquish control for the benefit of collaborating and sharing the work with others?

6) If you work with other people, what kind of operating structure will you have?

7) How will you fundraise?

8) Where will the money come from to start the project? How much are you willing to sink in?

9) Why do you want to do this?

10) How will your zine be sufficiently different from other, similar zines?

11) How will you spread the word about your project?

12) Will you continue to be interested in working on it if it isn't getting as much attention as you had initially hoped?

13) Do you honestly have the time and money to commit to it?

diy nike style: zines & the corporate world

By Stephen Duncombe

"Think! Think! It ain't illegal, yet!!" reads the first page of *U Don't Stop*, a zine I picked up the other day. It's not an unusual request.

Often hand-lettered, illustrated with cut and paste collages, and run off on photocopy machines, the message of the medium is that anyone can put one out. "The scruffier the better," argues Michael Carr, one of the editors of the punk zine *Ben is Dead*, because, "They look as if no corporation, big business or advertisers had anything to do with them." The anti-commercial ethos of the zine world is so commanding that writers who dare to move their project across the line into profitability—or at times even popularity—are reined in with the accusation of "selling out." In the shadows of capitalism, the zine world is busy creating a culture whose value isn't calculated as profit and loss on ruled ledger papers, but is assembled in the margins, using criteria like control, connection, and authenticity.

The search for authenticity drives the ethics of DIY. Against a world of pseudo-events and image consultants, zine writers are defining for themselves what's real. They use their zines to unleash an existential howl: I exist and here's what I think. *U Don't Stop* is a basketball zine; an intimate evocation of the street level scene which surrounds and sustains the game. Inside issue #2 there's a round up of the best public ball courts in Los Angeles, an interview with Munier, an African-American comic writer, and a tribute to the great funk musician George Clinton. B-ball related poetry and comics are salted throughout. *U Don't Stop*, like all zines, reads like a labor of love. One of the co-editors, Jimmy "Stank" Smith, sets the personal tone of the zine early with his hand scrawled introductory rant. In conventional scruffy zine style, with crossed off words kept in the text, he blasts out an impassioned plea for independent thought, ending his extemporaneous riff with the evocation: "Power." Indeed, it is a powerful testimonial of the irrepressible spirit of independent communication.

Well, maybe not. A little digging reveals that the two editors of *U Don't Stop*, Jimmy "Stank" Smith and John "Doc" Jay, are, in fact, copy writer and creative director, respectively, for the advertising firm of Wieden & Kennedy, the folks who sold sneakers to Gil Scott-Heron's "The Revolution Will Not Be Televised" and coined the famous DIY cry: "Just Do It!" Sure enough, the small print at the bottom of *U Don't Stop* reads ©1998 Nike Inc. This is DIY— Nike style.

Co-opting alternative culture, of course, is nothing new. Nike, adroit at strip-mining black youth culture for years, is actually a latecomer to the commercial harvest of the whiter alternative scene that zines represent. For years *Dirt* was a zine produced by the employees of the "Alternative Marketing" division of Warner records. The clothing chain Urban Outfitters churned out *Slant* (including a "punk rock" issue). The Body Shop printed up *Full Voice*, a zine lauding those who are "rebelling against a system that just won't listen" and encouraging others to do the same. Chris Dodge, professional librarian and zine bibliographer, estimates that there are dozens of these faux fanzines floating around out there.

What do corporations expect to reap in return from their zines? Not direct sales. Filled with the typical zine fare of rants, comics, interviews with musicians, and poetry, *U Don't Stop*—like most other astroturf zines—doesn't openly sell its patron's products. True, the street ball heroes of the zine's comic strip are wearing Nikes, and they've subsequently appeared on billboards in major urban markets, but this is low-key stuff. When I called Wieden & Kennedy's Jimmy Smith and asked him why the Nike logo was conspicuously absent from *U Don't Stop* he explained that, "The reason [the zine] is done without a swoosh is that kids are very sophisticated. It ain't like back in the day when you could do a commercial that showed a hammer hitting a brain: Pounding Headache. You know, it's gotta be something cool that they can get into." The goal is to create an association between the brand and "something cool they can get into," that is, a genuine grass-roots alternative culture. As David Rheins, former advertising director for *SPIN* Magazine, wrote in the trade journal *Mediaweek*, "It is not enough to merely package the right marketing message in a creative execution—it is necessary to deliver it in an environment that holds credibility with this audience." In more colloquial language Smith puts it this way: "If you've got them feeling you, you've won half the battle."

Advertisers, like zinesters, understand that commercial culture lacks authenticity. Built on instrumental market relationships— where people are considered a means to an end and not an end in themselves—capitalism is forever alienating the very individuals it relies upon to work, vote, and, in this case, buy. "Kids hate advertising," *U Don't Stop*'s Smith explain. "If they hate advertising and you're doing advertising, to me it sounds like you've got a little bit of a problem." Ironically, it's alternative culture like zines that offer a solution, providing a primary expression of people's lives and dreams: do-it-yourself authenticity. If properly packaged, the ideas, styles, and media of the underground provide material to renew and refresh the very culture they are created in opposition to. As *Business Week* reported in a special feature on new strategies in marketing, advertisers are now looking to "hide their corporate provenance." The report continues: "The idea is to fake an aura of colorful entrepreneurship as a way to connect with younger consumers who yearn for products that are hand-made, quirky, and authentic." An example *Business Week* offers of this fakery? No surprise: "mock 'zines'."

Many progressives—and zinesters—like to think of The System as a gray, pleasure-stomping behemoth. It is that. The rabble have to be kept in line and the best way to do this in a society where the jackboot is frowned on is to impose a uniform set of values and norms. The system is also something else: it's a consumer capitalist economy that depends on new ideas and new styles to open up new markets and sell more goods. "We track the movements among these progressive mind-sets," explains Janine Lopiano-Misdom and Joanne De Luca, co-founders of *The Sputnik Mindtrends Report* and authors of the recent *Street Trends: How Today's Alternative Cultures are Creating Tomorrow's Mainstream Markets*, "and interpret them into actionable opportunities for marketing, new product development, brand management and advertising." For the authors of *Street Trends*, anything and everything "progressive" becomes grist for the marketing mill, as chapter titles like "Positive Anarchy" and, you guessed it, "DIY: Do It Yourself," attest. In this environment, rebelling through culture means working as an unpaid intern for a market research firm.

But this sober realization needn't lead to a miserable fit of the blues. The dance continues, and faced with the discovery and commercialization of their culture, zine writers move on, some even poaching styles from the culture that stole from them. Carrie McLaren, for example, named her zine *Stay Free!*, pirating the name from a product that once promised women's liberation via the shining path of no-slide sanitary napkins. She's also picked up design tips from the slick, commercial magazines that Nike et al. are so desperate to distance themselves from. As Carrie points out, using a personal computer for desktop publishing means that it's actually easier to make her publication look "professional" than it is to replicate the old amateur aesthetic of zines. Besides, she adds, making her zine look nice means that more people will read what she has to say. This is important, for while the look of zines may be changing their message is not.

"I'm an asshole" reads the ad copy over a picture of a self-satisfied man showing off his sport utility vehicle on the back cover of *Stay Free!* #15, "And I've got the vehicle to prove it." From fake ads to interviews with media critics to a satirical quiz on how to "Test Your Book's Oprah Quotient" (Your protagonist is caught up in... A repressive political regime, -20 points; Problems at home, +50 points), *Stay Free!* mercilessly exposes, lampoons, and slaggs consumer culture from cover to cover. But in the spirit of DIY, the zine proposes something more: fighting the system. The tactic, however, that *Stay Free!* counsels is not retreat into some authentic subculture but moving out into the world, learning from the big boys, and employing the language and symbols that— for better or worse—constitute our lingua franca. Carrie and her friends, for example, staged a mock public salute to the Golden Marble children's advertising awards being held in New York City. Dressed as Goldie the Weasel, they handed out comic books "celebrating" the most egregious abuses of corporate America in their quest for the hearts and dollars of young people. As Carrie writes in her—carefully typeset—opening editorial in issue #14, "to fight a good fight you must access the enemy's power, and to see your own role in it, before deciding where to go from there."

Jean Railla, editor of the zine *Crafty Lady*, feels liberated by the direction that *Stay Free!* and her own—carefully crafted and digitally rendered—zine have gone, shifting emphasis away from preconceived style and toward what really matters: content and process. "It's not shocking to me that corporations are putting out fake zines. It makes total sense given the state of advertising in this culture."

"It used to make me sick; it was all the more reason to retreat into the subculture," Jean explains, acknowledging "this separatism really limited my scope and view of the world." "Now," she reflects, "I try to focus on saying what I want to say... and on the fact that girls out in the middle of Kansas still make zines for one another. The activity of making zines is what is really important—and all the marketing in the world cannot change that."

The left, like bohemia, has long held as an article of faith that certain stances, styles, and representations embody certain—progressive or conservative—politics. It's time to lose that religion. Sure, I'm disgusted by Nike's looting of my beloved zine culture, just as I shudder each time I hear "The Revolution Will Not Be Televised" as an ad jingle. But I also feel a curious sense of relief. The easy expropriation of even the most rebellious culture should

open our eyes to the fact that pat notions about the "politics of representation," "cultures of resistance," and "authenticity" are hopelessly outdated. In our free-wheeling, postmodern playhouse of a world: Image is Nothing. No, wait, that's the ad copy for a Sprite commercial.

Inspiration & Creativity

I grew up without any real security. My home life was violent and scary. It felt like every day could be my last. This turned me into an impulsive adult always creatively plodding forward without hesitation because, well, I had nothing to lose. This allowed me to be prolific as a writer without my forethought or afterthought stopping me mid-sentence. If I had an idea, I normally executed it right away! It's a double-edged sword, of course, but I never have any shortage of motivation or ideas. As a result, my early zines combined ideological political writing with bad puns about the names of countries and instructions for how to detonate sea gulls. But, for better or worse, there wasn't anyone to stop me and a cacophony of voices gradually and lovingly chimed in to offer feedback and suggestions. Now I crave security a bit more and am becoming a bit more methodical, realizing how it all looks and feels from the outside. At the same time, perfection is a myth. That's an important lesson about growing up as a zine writer: making mistakes publicly will cause others to be more invested in you and see you as an endearing case to watch in the future.

Granted, if meticulous grammar and spelling is your bread and butter and one of your most deeply held personal values, by all means, stick to them. But for most of us, they simply get in the way of expressing ourselves clearly. Write in the voice that comes naturally to you rather than the one that you think is "correct." More and more, making a zine is about donning a pair of colored glasses to view the world through and a way of interacting with others through that lens. You need to get yourself comfortably into that place.

Take off your shoes and loosen your clothes. Wear things that are physically and emotionally comforting. Stop what you are doing and sit still for a few minutes. Empty your mind of cares and worries. Every time you have a distracting thought, acknowledge it and let it go. Or maybe it's a good muse and writing prompt. Either way, before long ideas will flood into your brain. Your peace of mind is more important than any arbitrary deadline or time crunch. The more that you do this, the easier it gets.

It's a good idea to stand up and get a glass of water or go to the bathroom every hour and stretch. If you get stuck, take a few deep breaths, inhaling through the nose and exhaling through your mouth. Set a time limit and stick to it. Then do something to reward yourself. You do crappy work when you are tired. Something that works for me is alternating two hours of "work" with an hour of something fun. Decorate the mug that you drink out of while writing your zine and celebrate your achievements! Coffee and beer dehydrate you, making it harder to be present and write, but that doesn't stop most zinesters!

Periodically change your visual focus. Focus on something in the distance for a minute. This will help relax your eye muscles and thinking, and assist your productivity!

If you are excitedly mid-thought, hold onto that as a good place to continue the next day instead of starting by staring at a blank slate all over again.

Inspiration is the "A-ha!" excitement, like you are being pushed by an unknown force to accomplish a goal. Inspiration comes when you are receptive to it. Some people draw inspiration from quiet settings, whereas others get inspired by the adrenaline rush of a busy setting, like seeing tons of other people's work at a conference

or festival. Turn on some angry, wistful, or somber music. Find the music that captures the emotions that you are trying to channel in your writing or whatever gets your brain moving.

Michael T Perkins of *Section 8* says that it was started by Black artists in 1999 to "so we could show off our artwork, poetry, comics, and short stories to other artists in our neighborhood." Leathia Miller started *Plumplandia* zine because "We have such a rad and vibrant fat community here! I wanted to create an outlet for us and increase the visibility of fat folks in general! I really liked the idea of doing a zine because it sounded creative and fun and I always loved the riot grrl zines from the 90s." Ayun Halliday started a zine because she "was a downtown-style actor accustomed to creating low budget work, and having a baby sort of scotched that. I craved an audience of strangers for my creative work." According to Matthew Thompson, *Fluke* zine was inspired into existence because "[founder] Steve had a job at a frozen yogurt spot where a homeless man would come into the store and write numbers on a piece of paper, from one to twenty-seven. At the time, in Steve's mind, the guy was trying to teach himself how to write numbers. Steve observed this man having limited resources but attempting to better his life. This moved Steve, who felt stagnant in his life."[5]

Think back to your most profound or deeply emotional experiences. Place yourself back in those moments and you'll likely find no shortage of things to write about. Some people find inspiration from hanging out with their latest crush or spending personal time with someone else who is productive or engaging. Others derive inspiration from nature, a long bicycle ride, or taking a workshop. Literature of any kind, especially other people's zines, can be very

---

5 If you can't get enough of stories like this, Mike Gunderloy published a book, *Factsheet Five's Why Publish?*, collecting hundreds of answers to that question. Read it for free at: Zinebook.com/resource/whypublish.pdf

inspirational. Sometimes you just have a great idea, and who knows where it came from.

The most important thing is to just start writing something. Fix it later. Get your thoughts out for now. When I'm creatively stuck I like to write answers on Quora.com, as it's a lower stakes environment to get my brain moving. Doing something similar can help you work through a creative block.

Learning to nurture and develop your thoughts and ideas becomes easier over time. You can store your ideas mentally, but it's helpful to keep a notebook to collect your constant brainstorms. Forgetting a great idea is the worst!

Give your ideas a chance to develop; we're our own worst critics. That's why an idea folder works so well; it gives us a place to hide things until we're really ready to see how they work together.

Anyone who puts out more than a couple issues of a zine is bound to improve simply because they have the opportunity to make refinements to their original concept. With anything, you will improve through practice and experience.

copyright

Many years ago I designed a t-shirt with the words "Put the Fun Between Your Legs" surrounding a picture of a bicycle. I used it in Microcosm's advertising and printed shirts in my basement. It was flattering when people started to bootleg the design until major corporations began to do so. Fed up, I contacted the trademark office in 2015, only to find out that a Mr. Nathan Gray had already registered my design as a trademark. I spent hours on the phone with the Trademark Office in Washington, DC. How could Nathan Gray trademark something that is so clearly based on my work? Apparently he could by claiming to be unaware of my image that had now sold over 25,000 prints and had reached all corners of the global bicycle community. With no irony, Nathan Gray informed me that he was raising money for at-risk youth and had no time or interest in talking to me. Fortunately, Mr. Gray had filed his application incorrectly and it was rejected, allowing me to get credit for my own work. I wrote him another letter about how I had grown up as an at-risk youth and would be the perfect recipient of his funds. I wrote the whole story for *Taking the Lane* zine. At least Nathan Gray hasn't tried to steal my story.

Some zine authors worry about major corporations stealing their work. Speaking purely along the lines of the law, these are not things to be concerned about. As soon as a work is published, it is protected.

A **copyright** protects an original artistic or literary work—like your zine. Any work created after January 1, 1978, is automatically protected from the moment of its creation and is ordinarily given a term enduring for the author's life plus an additional 70 years after the author's death. If you love paperwork or believe that copyrighting your zine would be a fun thing to do, complete Form SE at copyright.gov/forms/ or simply print a copyright symbol on anything you suspect would be stolen. "All contents Copyright © [year] by [your name]" Sometimes people will mail a copy to themselves in order to have a post-marked date stamp. Leave the envelope sealed when it arrives. But when it comes down to it, if or when your peers are stealing your work, court is probably still not the best place to resolve any hard feelings.

You are copywriting the editing of your zine as a "literary" work. Contributors would continue to retain their copyright to their own work. If you really love federal agencies, send two copies of anything you publish to Register of Copyrights, Copyright Acquisitions Div., Library of Congress, Washington DC 20559-6000, which gives your work limited protection and ensures you that it's on a government shelf somewhere, which is amusing, especially if your zine is a collection of meandering anecdotes and run-on sentences. If you don't care to let the Library of Congress know what you're up to, then you don't have to.

On the other hand, if I were trying to decide whether I could use someone else's image, I wouldn't worry about anything over twenty-five years old. This is where protections end for printed materials. The trick is to watch out for if it has been re-published in that time period.

HINT: When in doubt, alter the image. This may still be considered "derivative," but should cover you if you change it enough. Three notable changes is considered standard. For instance, many artists use photos from magazines as references for their illustrations, but in the interpretation of a photo to a drawing, you could put the drawing right next to the photo and see little resemblance.

A **trademark** is a phrase, symbol, or design which identifies and distinguishes a company in advertising. It's the recognizeability of Nike's swoosh or the slogan on a ketchup bottle. A trademark must be used *in advertising* rather than only sold as a product. If "Put the Fun Between Your Legs" was only a t-shirt that I sold, I could not have trademarked it. I had to also use it on my work to tell people what my values were.

You cannot copyright a title but if you're thinking of trademarking the name of your zine, send me the money instead. On the other hand, zine publishers *do* get in trouble. Xerox contacted *Xerox Debt* and demanded that they change their name. It's now *Xerography Debt*. Mattel sent *Hey There, Barbie Girl* a cease-and-desist letter; the editor subsequently started a new zine without the word "Barbie" in it. After *Bunnyhop* featured a parody of a Matt Groening drawing on the cover, the publisher had to destroy all copies of it. Most people don't care but companies are forced to protect their trademarks or lose the rights to them. Disney, eBay, and Starbucks are notably litigous. Kieron Dwyer's *Lowest Common Denominator* showed an adapted Starbucks logo parody with the new text "Corporate Whore" and was promptly sued for trademark infringement because they argued that the parody resembled the actual logo to the average person.

When it comes down to it, the corporation usually wins—through sheer volume of resources. Of course, it's okay to use an image that *evokes* the character you have in mind as long as the "average person" would not be likely to mistake your use as representing the actual brand or its trademarks. The axiom "it's only illegal if someone notices" may apply here.

There are newer provisions in copyright thinking for "Creative Commons" and Copyleft that are more in line with the ethics of most zines. Copyleft originated as a new way of looking at legal protections and rights for software around 1975. Programmers wanted their code to be used by other people, improved, modified, and shared—requiring that the same freedoms be applied to future modified versions. You can determine what other people can do with your work and vice versa.

Copyleft allows the creator to impose some but not all copyright restrictions on those who want to engage in activities that would otherwise be considered copyright infringement. Under copyleft, usage infringement may be avoided if the would-be infringer continues the same copyleft arrangement. Because of this, copyleft licenses are also known as viral or reciprocal licenses.

Copyleft frequently includes a non-commercial clause, meaning that anyone can reuse your work as long as it's not for-profit. This way it keeps the work within a certain community.

There are six variations of Creative Commons licensing:
1. Attribution (You must state who it was originally by)
2. Attribution + Noncommercial Use
3. Attribution + NoDerivs (You cannot change the original)
4. Attribution + ShareAlike (You can change and distribute a deriviative version)
5. Attribution + Noncommercial + NoDerivs
6. Attribution + Noncommercial + ShareAlike

The Rad Possibilities of Creative Commons
By Katie Haegele

The other day I downloaded a philosophy class from MIT's website. All the course materials were free to me, even though I'm not a student—the readings list, the professor's notes, even the slide presentations. The reason I could do this is because MIT has published most of the content of almost all its classes as "OpenCourseWare" under a non-commercial, share alike, attribution copyright. This means, basically, that we can all look at and share the materials for free as long as we don't profit from them and give the proper attribution if we reproduce or quote from them. They don't even ask you to register. They're just giving it away.

As a writer, zinester, and reader, new ideas about creative ownership really excite me. It seems to me that these changes could mean all kinds of good things to us writers and artists, allowing us to disseminate our work further and share it more fully. Maybe it will ultimately help break the back of the ownership structure that the mainstream publishing world is built on, too. Wouldn't *that* be nice.

Ironically, I first started making zines because of a copyright question. A good few years ago I got really into making found poetry; everywhere I looked I saw a poem. Found poems are a kind of word collage, and to make one you use text that already exists— say, the owner's manual of an oven—and rearrange it in such a way that the words take on new meanings. What you're really doing is seeing the poetry that's already there and helping others to see it too. I'll give you an example. I made a poem from the Orienteering section of the 1948 edition of the *Boy Scout Handbook*, which I must have found at some rummage sale. "Find Your Way" was the name of the section, and that's what I called the poem. "With simple means/ and using your own personal measurements,/ determine a height you cannot reach/ and a width you cannot walk./ Call loudly for help if you are alone,/ and keep on calling." The book was talking about how to save yourself if you got lost in the woods, but it felt like a poem to me.

I wanted to share these poems with other people but I wasn't sure how. Wouldn't there be copyright problems if I tried to publish them? The Boy Scout book was old but some of my other sources were current, such as a list of movie titles from the Lifetime Television network. (Now *there* was a comic-poetry treasure trove.) For a while I didn't know what to do with my poems so I just carried them around in a notebook that I kept adding to obsessively. Then I remembered: zines! I'd always wanted to make a zine but hadn't known what I'd write about. These eccentric poems seemed like a good bet. I collected my favorite ones and asked an artist named Lesley Reppeteaux whose work I really like to make a drawing for the cover. I called the little collection *Word Math* and in all the years I've been making zines I've never stopped selling it.

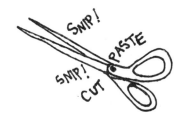

Take the beautiful logic of found poetry a step further. What if people wrote things that they *wanted* other people to pass on or recycle in some way? Think of the ripple effect your work would have if you released it into the wild and it just kept going, getting turned into poems, appearing in other people's zines, being read into a microphone at a reading in some city you've never been to. My friend Roger Simian, an inventive soul from Scotland, wanted to include me in an issue of his zine *dumb/SULK trigg-er*. He decided the best way to tell people what my writing is like was to make a word salad out of it, stringing together sentences from poems, essays, and stories I'd written. They were my words but it was his story—his story of me. In this way his reading of someone else's writing became its own piece of writing. That's collaboration of a very powerful kind, a kind of consummation of the connection that's always made between writer and reader. I gave him permission to play with my writing like that, but what if I gave the whole world permission? It seems like the very idea of what it means to be an author could start to change. I get excited thinking about the new places we DIY publishers can go. Don't you?

On Libel

I n 2004 Microcosm announced that we were going to publish a little zine called *On Subbing*. Soon we received our first threatening letter—from the school board that was being written about—and the author, still a teacher at the school, was informed that he could not relate his experiences because it would libel staff or students. Not being college educated, I had to look the word up. It means "damaging to a person's reputation." We found a very nice lawyer who explained that if we anonymized people's identities, we should be fine. I swear that every employee of the school district must have come by our office to buy copies of the zine and see if they were mentioned in it.

In reality, situations like this are very rare. In the thirteen years since then, we received a cease-and-desist letter about mentioning

Dr. Seuss' *The Lorax* character, as the family believed that we were diminishing the value of the intellectual property by equating it with social justice environmental activism. They seemed more powerful than the school board so we agreed to stop.

You will probably never experience anything similar to either of these situations unless you really like to look for trouble.

To prove something is libelous, someone must prove that all of these aspects are true:

1) Defamatory language was used.

2) Defamatory language refers to the person in question. A person doesn't have to be named if identifying details are sufficient.

3) Defamatory language was published.

4) The language damaged the person's reputation.

Number four can be the stickiest since the law has the most loopholes. In the United States, expressing your opinion is legal. Opinions cannot be proven wrong so if you publish something that can be proven wrong, you are likely liable for it.

In 1983, the *Altoona Telegraph* sent a letter to the U.S. Department of Justice (DOJ), asking if organized crime money was going to a particular construction company. DOJ sent a memo to federal bank regulators, and the bank canceled the builder's line of credit. The construction company sued, the accusation proved false, and the newspaper was guilty of libel because it sent the accusatory letter to the DOJ, which damaged the company's reputation.

You can say that a restaurant is "gross," because that's an opinion; a value judgment. You can't prove or disprove that it's "gross." You can't claim that a restaurant has health code violations unless that is true. Even if the only reason that they don't is because they don't open until the health inspector goes home for the day, you can only state the facts of the matter without showing causation.

You cannot legally call someone an alcoholic, abusive, or insane because those words mean something, even if you don't mean their denotative meaning in your hyperbolic use. In this case, it's safer to call them an "asshole," as it's a matter of opinion. Stick to outrageous hyperbole. It's funnier and no one will read it as fact. Say "That guy was such an asshole that even a used car salesman ran away from him in terror!" People will get your meaning.

Most people also have a right to privacy, *except* public figures. They are responsible to tolerate a higher level of scrutiny as part of the democratic system. This is why you can say that Donald Trump is an egomaniacal sexual predator who is hell-bent on destroying America even if you cannot prove that he did any of these things.

Public figures include people elected to public office, most public employees, and people with a certain amount of fame or people who voluntarily involve themselves in public controversies, like Jane Fonda, The Octomom, L. Ron Hubbard, Kanye West, Taylor Swift, and Angelina Jolie. Just because a person is central and important in your universe does not make them a public figure. People criticizing me have argued that *I* am a public figure, and thus subject to public scrutiny. But do your neighbors know who I am? Do your parents? How many social media followers does the person have? (I only have 800). Gary Johnson *might* be considered a public figure for purposes of the 2016 Presidential election, but he'll be forgotten in time. When *Rolling Stone* speculated about the divorce of Against Me! frontwoman Laura Jane Grace, her status as a public figure was borderline.

People accused of crimes, like Cliven Bundy, who occupied the federal nature preserve in Oregon, are not public figures, especially if they are found innocent. By keeping to themself, they avoid becoming a "public figure." Of course, you can still call Bundy an asshole.

Similarly, parody is protected speech. The *Onion* ran the story "Black Man Given Nation's Worst Job" when Obama was elected. Microcosm published *Henry & Glenn Forever,* a fictional account of Rollins and Danzig jealously engaging in couple's spats. They are funny because they point to larger truths without mischaracterizing the facts.

I'm willing to bet that you make a zine to express your opinions. Stick to that and provable facts and you'll be fine.

contributors

The day that I brought my first issue of *Stink in Public* with me to high school I had dozens of people asking to write and draw for the second issue. From there I had strangers mailing me submissions ranging from interviews to photos to illustrations to editorials to political essays. I loved it. Then a contributor's copies fell apart in the mail and neither of us wanted to pay to replace them. We didn't really have a plan or agreement in place for a situation like that. I learned the value of managing expectations and treating people that wanted to help with my zine with respect. I began sending out contributor copies before orders and built a hierarchy of who was most invested in the zine and should feel important. I managed relationships with everyone as much as possible. This led all of us to become more invested and excited to work together. Knowing each other helped us have better ideas of how to work together.

Know what you want. Just like a party, if you only invite affluent, able-bodied, white males, those will be the people who show up. To have a true diversity of voices, you have to tell people what you want. "We try to include everything that is submitted. We really want to keep the zine specific to Portland and the fat community here. If we aren't sure, we discuss it as a team and decide," says Leathia Miller of *Plumplandia*. Brown Recluse Zine Distro exclusively sells zines by people of color so you know exactly what they offer. Microcosm's own submission guidelines state "we double the industry standard in women authors...people of color are particularly encouraged to submit as is anyone whose experiences are not represented in the publishing world." I felt a little weird about this at first because it felt tokenizing, like it was these signifying statuses we were seeking more than substance or ideas. But in our internal conversations, I came to believe that if we don't outwardly and intentionally project that we are explicitly seeking these things, people will assume that we are upholding a microcosm of the sexism, racism, ableism, and classism that exists everywhere else in the world. In practice our submission habits give preference based on merit, substance, and following directions but putting up these flags increased the numbers of both women and people of color who submit.

Elly Blue, editor of the feminist bike zine *Taking the Lane*, allows men to contribute but does not publish sexist submissions. That doesn't mean that she doesn't receive them. Similarly, there are so many authors and artists in the world with so much to express that you shouldn't ever take submissions that you don't like or contradict the mission of your zine. It's satisfying for the contributors to see their work in print and have it read and commented on. Of course, sometimes you'll have to work with an author to turn their story into something great or highlighting elements that makes it a better fit for your zine. If there is someone that you'd like to have as a contributor, don't be afraid to ask. They may decline, but often times even notable writers are happy to get involved in a passion project. Contrary to belief, people with less experience tend to try harder or at least rely on their editor less.

Sometimes things don't work out. A contributor could be difficult or demanding to work with; someone could beg for deadline extensions and never submit. Don't hold a grudge. It's part of working with people on a passion project. If a contributor is consistently flaky, you don't need to put up with that.

You should acknowledge that, unless you are paying $50 or more per item, you are essentially relying on volunteer labor. Promoting your contributors' other projects is a nice way of acknowledging your appreciation for them. If you can afford to pay a little, great. If you can't, be up-front about this from the beginning.

You'll receive submissions you don't want to print. Some editors write personal rejection notes. Some send cold, professional rejections. If you do, scribble an encouraging and constructive line or two to personalize and energize your correspondence. These days, I prefer not to respond to rejected pieces to avoid hurt feelings and protracted, defensive arguments with the contributor about why they feel they should be included.

diy comix
By Fly

Your DIY Comix can be true to your ideals and vision. You can use self-publishing experiments to develop ideas to pitch later to a publishing house as a complete book. A lot of artists have self-published before getting deals with established publishers. Some examples are Julie Doucet, Adrian Tomine, Peter Kuper, and Eric Drooker. A lot of the underground cartoonists of the '60s put out their own magazines and created a revolution within the comics industry. R. Crumb put together a comic with his brother when they were just kids. Jerry Seigel—creator of Superman—put out his first fanzine in 1929 called *Cosmic Stories*. This was one of the first of a wave of science fiction fan publications. For an insightful and fact-filled background on the history of comics, read *Men of Tomorrow* by Gerard Jones.

Story Ideas & Scripting

A lot of DIY comix are based on personal stories, but this doesn't have to be the case. You can create a story based on fact or fiction or any mix of the two. Sometimes you might want to tell a story based on a true event but change the characters slightly so as not to embarrass, incriminate, or otherwise expose real individuals. You may want to change the sequence or details of events in order to

allow the story to flow better. You may want to write a story where you are the main character, but you don't want it to be so personal, so you change the "I" character to a third person character. For example, I do a series of comics based on a "fictional" character called K9. The stories depicted are based on real-life events that I experienced but I have changed some details of the story so it would all make sense without going into too many personal details. I feel that if I was representing it as "absolute truth," I would have to be more conscious of following the facts to the letter. In this case I didn't want to be tied down to all the details and complications that this would entail.

I created a comic about my first 24 hours in NYC, using a character, the Goddess Garbage, to represent myself. I also had another character who was based on a real person, and although I didn't use his actual name, he visually resembled the real guy. The comic had lots of funny details about rough squats and piss buckets and junkies having fits. It was published in the *New York Press*, the guy saw it, and recognized himself immediately, and he got so pissed off at me! He used to yell at me on the street for years after that. This is what can happen when you put real-life characters into your comics. They might not always like how they're portrayed.

There are cases where following the facts to the letter is an integral part of the story. Some political comics, like Joe Sacco's *Palestine* and *Safe Area Gorazde*—both deal with exposing the real-life political situation and personal conflicts within war zones. Sacco is a journalist as well as a comics artist, and his work is informative, educational, and necessary. Seth Tobocman's work is another example of political comics that work to convey real-world situations. His book *War in the Neighborhood* recounts the conflict between squatters and real estate development sympathizers in the Lower East Side of NYC. His work is his own personal story of involvement as an activist in the struggle for housing. Tobocman is also a co-founder of *World War 3 Illustrated*, which is an example of collective self-publishing—a collection of work by political cartoonists, writers, and illustrators that has been coming out since 1980.

Another interesting place to get ideas for stories is from your dreams. It can be very useful and inspirational to keep a dream journal. If you keep a notebook and pen by your bed, you can train yourself to jot down notes immediately upon waking or even in the middle of the night. I have done several comics based entirely on dreams (with a little tweaking to make it flow into a "story"). They make great stories even if they are a little abstract.

Scripting

There are a lot of different approaches to scripting. Although The *DC Comics Guide to Writing Comics* by Dennis O'Neil mainly deals with the idea of writing superhero comics, he has good points on plot and character development and reprints examples of different approaches to scripting, from simple notes to detailed, page-by-page, panel-by-panel breakdowns of narrative, dialog and descriptions of action. Such detailed scripts might be provided when a writer and artist are working together yet independently on a project. In the "Industry" it is common to have the writer, editor, penciller, inker, colorist, and letterer be different people.

Starting

Dennis O'Neil has some good tips about comic story writing. He recommends that you know the end of the story before you write the beginning. He divides the story structure into three acts: Act one is the "hook", *an inciting incident that establishes the situation and conflict*. This action could also be translated visually as a "splash" page, *a full page of visual action to introduce the reader to the story and excite their interest*. Act two is the meat of your story, the development and complication of situations. Act three is the events leading to a climax. Then comes the denouement, the winding up, or resolution of the story.

- The plot and sub-plots are the action of the story advancing toward a resolution
- Character development supports the plot—you might have a hero and an anti-hero (or antagonist) and other supporting characters
- Think of the motivations of your character:
- What does he/she want?
- What or who does he/she love?
- What is he/she afraid of?
- Why does he/she involve him/herself in situations?

A Fly comic about cement-mixing that needed to be accurate.

All of these points are not hard and fast rules, but they are useful to keep in mind in order to keep a focus to your story. What are you trying to communicate? You might want to write a personal story like a journal or a recounting of a specific event. In that case, the way the story tells itself is often similar to the approach O'Neil describes in creating fictional stories. There is usually some sort

of protagonist and antagonist, resulting in some kind of conflict; exciting or interesting events unfold, and then there is a resolution.

To start, it is a good idea to keep it simple and to the point. Don't get sidetracked or bogged down by too many distracting details. Focus on what is important to the story. Begin by outlining the main events or "beats" of the story. This can help estimate the number of pages and possibilities for panel breakdowns. You can use Post-its or index cards or a computer at this stage. Once you get the basic plot laid out, you can use this as your outline and go straight to sketching out "thumbnails" (miniature versions of your page layout), or you could write a more detailed script.

My personal version of scripting is extremely loose. Usually I have the story written. For example, my comic *Meanwhile* was based on a dream I had written down. I knew my page count, so I went through the story and divided the action into different pages and then started drawing. However, in my Mother Jones comic, Trina Robbins wrote the script. Because the comic had to be as historically accurate as possible, I was thankful for her detailed panel-by-panel descriptions and directions.

Thumbnails & Sketches
Once you have your story or script written and before you start sketching, there are some important things you need to know:
How many pages will you be working with?
What is the size or dimension of those pages?

Thumbnails
Once you figure out your dimensions and page count it's time to start considering how the story will be translated with art onto the page. Many artists do thumbnails at this point—*miniature*

versions of the page where you can experiment with different layout designs and panel configurations. This may help you refine how your story will be broken down into separate pages. It can help you establish your pacing and sense of time and space.

Character Research

Before you start doing your sketches, it might be useful to do some preliminary work, especially if you are working on a story that is based on real events. Research of images and settings is very effective to create a sense of "realism." Even if your art is not "realistic," if it is based on actual research you might be able to create a more convincing imaginary reality and will avoid getting

basic facts wrong. Of course your story might be based purely on fantasy. Even so, if you can practice drawing from life it will help you manipulate your images in a way that you might be better able to communicate your story without the art becoming too confusing or unrecognizable. For example, I did a comic based on a dream that I had where I crossed a bridge. Although it was a dream sequence and all the lines were warped, I based the images on some sketches I had done of bridges.

Character Design

It can also be very beneficial to do some preliminary sketches to develop your characters. This can help you practice drawing your characters from all angles and still keep them consistent and consistency will help your readers to follow the story. If one character looks different in every panel then it will become confusing. Similarly if all of your characters look the same it will be hard to follow the story. Developing the character is very important in stories that are based on real people. For example, in Seth Tobocman's comic about Mumia Abu Jamal, an African-American journalist on death row for decades, it was essential that Tobocman study Mumia and practice drawing him before doing the comic. Anything less may have undermined the credibility of the story.

If you work on your character development, you will be more confident when it comes to putting the final sketches together and this will help you communicate more effectively to your readers. Even if you are doing very cartoony and simplified drawings, it helps to practice drawing from life. It will help you in making your characters more animated and relatable to the reader.

Page Design

To me, this is one of the hardest steps—starting to visualize your story—there are just so many possibilities! It's up to you to create your own visual vocabulary and present it within a believable sense of time and space.

A few components to keep in mind are:

Clarity (what is the point or focus of your story?)

Realism (Can the reader believe in your "world"?)

Dynamism (keeping it interesting and full of life)

Continuity (backgrounds, character appearance, "axis of action" or direction of action and "props").

Deciding what to illustrate and what to break down into dialog and how to compose it all so it works fluidly is a skill that you will develop with experience. You can use your intuition to great effect during this process to figure out what works and what doesn't. What kind of images and in what order do you need to get your story across? What should you illustrate, what should be conveyed in dialogue, and what should be a caption? It's superfluous to write a caption saying "he walked upstairs" and then have a picture of a guy walking upstairs. There are many different ways to combine words and images to create a comic.

Scott McCloud breaks it down in *Understanding Comics* as follows:
Word specific—images illustrate text
Picture specific—mainly visual sequence
Duo specific—both image and text in equal balance
Additive—words amplify or elaborate image (or vice versa)
Parallel—words and image follow different tracks simultaneously
Montage—like collage—words as visual element
Interdependent—words and pictures work together to convey an idea that neither could convey alone

People in the West generally read a page from left to right and top to bottom. If your panels are arranged to flow in any other odd configuration, make sure that this is clear, or you could end up confusing your reader and distracting them from the story.

As you figure out your page layout, keep in mind a sense of timing. Using a grid pattern of panels (all equal size) can somewhat neutralize the reader's sense of time passing. Using different shapes and configurations of panels can reinforce the sense of time and space. A stretched-out panel might indicate more time passing or create a sense of more space. A panel containing an inset panel with a close-up might indicate an almost instantaneous action. You can affect the sense of timing with the space in between panels. The panels should work coherently together to move your story forward.

Scott McCloud defines this idea as "closure", "the phenomenon of observing the parts but perceiving the whole." I recommend taking a look at his book *Understanding Comics* for an in-depth discussion of the concept of the panel and how to use it.

Another great reference book is Will Eisner's *Comics & Sequential Art*. Eisner was a master storyteller and much of his compositional work is pure genius.

Some points he makes about using panels are:

Panel borders—need not always be straight lines. They can be used to indicate flashbacks or dreams; for example, they could also indicate emotional content. Jagged edges may give the feeling of danger or agitation. The lack of borders may indicate a sense of unlimited space and may give the audience the opportunity to create the background with their imaginations.

Framing—the panel borders could become a structural element of the story, for example, a doorway or a window.

Panel composition—when considering your panel composition, keep in mind the focus point and consider continuity with other panels. Establish a sense of perspective and then embellish.

Perspective within the panel can manipulate the reader's orientation and affect emotional states as well as convey information. An overhead view may give the reader a feeling of

being more detached. Eye level views may let the audience feel more involved and make the action seem more immediate. A ground level view might create more of a sense of vulnerability in the reader.

However you arrange your panels and create your compositions, try to keep in mind the information and emotion you are trying to convey—is it relevant to your story? Is it moving your story forward in a coherent and interesting way?

Klaus Janson's *The DC Comics Guide to Penciling Comics* details all the steps and considerations involved in creating comics art from a script. When structuring pages and panels he recommends considering:

Eye Movement—more eye movement might create more excitement and interest. Is your focal point in the center of every panel or are you moving it around?

Contrast—contrast of shapes and sizes as well as black and white)

Balance (symmetrical or asymmetrical?)

The Diagonal—designing the action or the figures on diagonals can add a more dynamic feeling and create more depth.

Janson goes on to describe the different kinds of "shots and angles" that are effectively used in comics:

Establishing shot—often at the beginning to establish the setting.

Extreme long shot—for example, a cityscape. It could also be used as an establishing shot.

Long shot—characters may be visible but do not dominate the setting.

Full shot—full length of body shown with the background secondary to characters.

Medium shot—maybe about half the body of the character. Background is simplified or non-existent.

Close-up—character from the top of the shoulders to the top of the head. Background is simplified or nonexistent.

Extreme close-up—character's face or part of the face fills the panel. Brings the reader right into the action.

It's a good idea to use variety depending on the needs of your story. The information and emotion you are trying to convey should affect the focus, perspective and composition of your panels. Remember to try to keep it directionally consistent. If your character is facing or moving in a certain direction in one panel, make sure you maintain that orientation in the following panel. If you mix it up you might end up confusing your reader.

My Comix Experience

When I first started making comix, I tried to make each page like a painting with all the action flowing together—I had no concept of "panels." I plan out my pages in my head and just start drawing. This worked sometimes, but sometimes it didn't. As I continued drawing comix I became better at actually planning a page and I even used panels! I would also do some preliminary sketches of the places I was trying to depict. Eventually I started working on comix that were based on real events and to me the details of the story were very important, as well as the images. I was using a lot of words. Some of the aspects of the stories were really intense.

an establishing shot from Fly's **K-9's First Time: The Boyfriend**

an extreme close up shot from the same story

For example, incidents of physical and sexual abuse. I didn't want to make it harder for the reader to ingest the story, so I tried to arrange things in a straightforward, very legible way. I didn't want to trivialize the content by making the compositions too "arty" or hard to read. I found using actual panels more efficient in getting my point across.

Usually I skip the thumbnail stage, but I do rough sketches at full size to figure out my page layout and what text I will include. Then I will sometimes lay out the panels with the captions on the computer in Indesign. Then I print out the pages and do the final sketches on the printouts. But I don't always use the computer to lay out the pages. Sometimes I will just draw the whole thing freehand, especially if I am including unusual panel shapes. After that, I transfer the sketches onto a light, smooth Bristol. These would be my final pencils. The next step would be inking.

It's a good idea to always carry a sketchbook with you, even a small one. You never know when you will see a person or a place that will either inspire you to create a new character or setting, or help you work on developing your current ideas. Many times you will see something or think of something and you'll think it's so obvious that you will remember it, but then later it's gone! Tragedy!

Final Art & Inking:

Figure out the process you want to use in going from your rough sketches to final art and inking. It's good to keep a few things in mind. Make sure that all your dimensions and page counts are correct. If you've made a mistake, now is the time to catch it. Once you're happy with your sketches you could ink directly on your drawings, however there are several disadvantages to this. Rough sketches tend to be just that, rough, with lots of pencil lines. Therefore it might be hard to erase after inking. The ink could smear, the paper could rip and some of the pencil lines may be so dark that they show up in the printing process.

Final Pencils

When I first started doing comix I used pens and inked directly on my first sketches. This method works but I found as I continued doing comix that it was better to do a stage of finished pencils from the sketches. It improved the drawing. I was able to refine it and the difference was noticeable. Also, it keeps your originals in good condition, maybe to reprint them at a later date or to show or sell them—they age better if you put them on better paper.

I also stopped using pens for the most part and ink mainly with a brush and Sumi ink. I found that using a brush and ink gave me a cleaner, more tapered line (the pen line always seems a little fuzzy to me). Also, it allowed more fluidity. I felt it easier to get a sense of movement within the drawing by using the brush.

Usually I transfer my rough sketches to the Bristol using a light table. If you don't have access to a light table, you can tape your original sketch up to a window during the day and tape the Bristol over that, and you have a natural light table. Another option is to get a piece of Plexiglas and put it over a milk crate with a clamp light beneath it. This works ok except that the light heats up the plexi and makes it a little warped. I have had problems with the ink refusing to adhere properly to the paper from greasiness so I usually wear a cotton glove on my drawing hand.

The size you do your final art is up to you, as long as the dimensions are correct. I used to try to do all my final art a little bigger than the print size would be. Often the art looks better and tighter when you reduce it. But you also have to consider your production techniques. Will you be scanning your art? If it's too big and won't fit on the scanner, then you will have to scan it in sections and stitch it together in Photoshop. These days, I try to work in a format that will fit my scanner, so I don't have to do that (though sometimes it's unavoidable). I usually work either at 100% or slightly larger (if the print size is smaller than 8.5"x11")

Inking

There are various methods and approaches to inking final art. Making DIY comix is a good opportunity to experiment with different materials and styles. The mood and content of your story can also be an indicator for how you will approach inking it. If your art is very geometric, then a Rapidograph pen might be a good option for you. If you want a dark engraved look, then you might want to try scratchboard. To achieve a more painterly and fluid line, you could use a brush. Of course, all of these mediums are capable of expressing a wide range of emotions and ideas in how you use them. You can also combine methods. It's a good idea to check out other comix and see how other artists have approached similar materials.

Some of the more popular inking techniques include
Disposable pens
Brush pens
Rapidograph pens
Crow quill pens
Brush and ink
Scratch board (comes in black or white)

I have also done final artwork using watercolor pencils and collage and ink together. This looked great when it was printed in a glossy magazine, but it didn't work so well when I included it in a photocopied zine. If you are using washes or tones, I recommend scanning your originals and doing your layout on the computer, so that you don't have to deal with copies of copies when you produce your zine. For a photocopied zine, I have found that straight black and white is the easiest to work with and gives the best results.

Paste Up and Production

When working on photocopied zines, you have to keep in mind the limitations and abilities of a photocopier when you are preparing your work. You are limited to copying on 8.5x11 or 8.5x14 or 11x17 size paper—if you want your zine to be a different size, you will have to trim it after it has been copied.

If your originals are larger than the size of your masters, then you could reduce them on a photocopier, or scan them and print them at a reduced size. Of course, if you are doing all of your layout on the computer, you will have to scan all of your artwork. If your art is line art, you can easily use photocopy reductions to do your paste up, but if you have used gray tones in your originals, you should probably scan them and print them out as halftones or use a photocopier that reproduces grays well. If your originals are the same size as your masters will be, you

FLY·2K3

could photocopy straight from them. You just have to make sure the layout is in the correct order.

Recommended Reading

Understanding Comics by Scott McCloud
Comics & Sequential Art by Will Eisner
Graphic Storytelling and Visual Narrative by Will Eisner
The DC Comics Guide to Writing Comics by Dennis O'Neil
Men of Tomorrow (a history of comics) by Gerard Jones
Writing for Comics with Peter David
The DC Comics Guide to Penciling Comics by Klaus Janson
The Art of Comic Book Inking—vol. 1 & 2 by Gary Martin
The DC Comics Guide to Penciling Comics by Klaus Janson

Read Comics By

Seth Tobocman, Joe Sacco, Eric Drooker, Peter Kuper, Will Eisner, Mary Fleener, Kim Deitch, Sabrina Jones, Megan Kelso, Abby Denson, Sophie Crumb, Alexandar Zograf, Mac McGill, Art Spiegelman, Windsor McKay, Cristy Road, Liz Baillie, Dori Seda, Gabrielle Bell, Jennifer Camper, The Hernandez Brothers, Peter Bagge, Gary Panter, Charles Burns, Dan Clowes, Moebius, Marjane Satrapi, Fiona Smyth, Carel Moiseiwitsch, Phoebe Glockner, Carrie McNinch, Aline Kominsky-Crumb, Leslie Sternbergh, Nicole Shulman, Trina Robbins (has written several books on the history of women in comics), Howard Cruse, Sue Coe

SO, TELL ME YOUR BIGGEST FEAR...

interviews

The only interview in the first issue of *Stink in Public* was done courtesy of William Rupnik, now an esteemed gallery owner in Cleveland. Of course, he didn't know that he was providing this interview for my zine as it was pilfered from his bedroom by his sister. He was upset when he saw it in print and I was confused as to why. Apparently, he had conducted it for a zine that never saw the light of day and then put the tape under his bed for a few years where it was unknowingly stolen and appeared in my zine. I didn't know that he hadn't given permission and in later issues, I did my own dirty work—ahem, interviews. For example, in my punk business issue, I interviewed people whose work I respected about their awkward navigations between punk and capitalism.

Interviews are a wonderful way to add variety to your zine, convey a point in a stronger way, tell a story that wouldn't otherwise be believable, or attract readers who are excited about a certain person, band, subculture, or organization.

There are typically two kinds of interviews. One is to profile an interesting personality, band, or organization; the other is to get quotes or perspective from a credible source to substantiate points you want to make. Interviews allow you to have someone else making or substantiating your points. It also makes for interesting reading when you have several people with different points of view.

In the mid-90s hey-day of zines, it was very common to find throwaway quality interviews with popular indie bands. The questions frequently lacked depth or thought, and the discussion would wind down as soon as it went anywhere. But your interviews can be as fascinating as your imagination.

In *Identity Crisis,* Lauren interviews a dozen of her peers who have extensive knowledge and experience in the punk scene—creating a composite of different lifestyles within our subculture. The long-running *Duplex Planet* interviews elderly people living in retirement homes and prints their acquired wisdom. *Cometbus* has featured interview issues with New York City cartoonists, employees of a worker-owned coffee shop, and children of the back-to-the-land movement.

Slave to the Needles interviews popular indie rockers, but only asks questions about their knitting and related crafts. It creates unique interviews with a familiar personality.

There are typically four ways to do an interview—in person, over the phone, by writing letters, or via e-mail.

E-mail is the least labor intensive as you can edit and paste the finished results right into your zine. Letter writing is typically reserved for subjects that have no other way of being interviewed (they live far away with no phone or e-mail). In-person interviews are best for understanding the nuances of your subject and playing off their non-verbal responses. It also offers the best opportunities for follow-up, conversation-style questions. Telephone interviews are easier to schedule than in-person interviews and can offer similar results. They are also good for follow-up interviews.

Familiarize yourself with the subject's work and read other interviews they've given. Run a basic Google search online and see what background facts you can find. Going in prepared and informed will help you to be confident.

Prepare six to ten questions ahead of time, and leave room for some degree of spontaneity. You don't want to sound like you're reading from a script and not acknowledging their responses. I normally add another six to ten questions during the course of the interview to help it feel more conversational.

Try to get a quiet setting for the interview; it eliminates background noise. Be on time. If you must be late, then call. Try to estimate how much time it'll take in advance and stick to it. You want to respect other people's time.

If you are recording by phone or in person, running a quick level check on the recorder is important. It only takes a minute or two. You don't want to take someone's time taping an interview, only to find out that everything is inaudible and useless. Learn how to use the recording feature on your phone before you rely on it for an interview. Let the subject do most of the talking, unless they need direction or you have something really compelling to say.

Sometimes the best material comes from discussing things that have nothing directly to do with your subject's vocation or main interest: upbringing, hobbies, popular music and TV shows. By straying from the beaten path, you may help to portray a warmer, more thoughtful side of a personality than most readers have seen.

You will get a better result when both you and the subject are relaxed, unless your point is to make your subject uncomfortable, like a politician or police officer.

Paraphrasing what your subject just said can help both of you focus. It can also help them clarify their points. Sometimes you'll want to use this method to allow them to have the most developed version of their thoughts and the simplest phrasing. This makes for the best quotes.

When the zine comes out, send a thank-you note and a copy to your subject.

organization

My records are organized geographically. This makes sense to me as each region has a certain sound and it creates an easy thematic transition from one band to another with similar roots and sound. Of course, when a former roommate could not find the record she was looking for, she declared my system "stupid" and proceeded to make fun of the way that I think. But it wasn't a system that was designed for her. It was designed to work for mc, and it does.

Your zine is more likely to be fun and stress-free if your space is organized. Whether your space is an actual room, a desk, the floor of your bedroom, the corner of a garage, or a combination of a laptop and the local copy place, you need a system for retrieving important things in a timely manner. It pays to set up this system early on. It's okay for your space to be cluttered or crowded, as long as you can find things when you need them.

Mail. If you're getting a lot of letters, orders, or submissions, you need some way to organize them, or at least keep them together until you have time to respond. You could "file" them all in a Postal Service mail tub, place them in file folders in a milk crate, transcribe them into a notebook, or create an Excel or database system on your computer. Maybe you intend to deal with each submission, order, and letter as it arrives, but it often proves to be an impossible ideal. The important thing is to keep everything in one place until it's time to deal with it. And to create a system that works for you. *Fluke*, a zine publishing since 1989 about Little Rock punk, has paste-up originals in folders from over 25 years ago. Ayun Halliday of *East Village Inky* manages her "subscribers, press contacts and distros with an app called Bento. If readers purchase subscriptions or individual issues via credit card, I am able to look up their info that way."

Use a tray, excel file, or computer program to organize chronologically what is owed you, and a different one for what you owe others. This way, you can tell at a glance when something is due. When a bill comes in, mark the back of the envelope with the amount to pay, and the date to pay it, factoring in enough days to allow for mail delivery. If you have zines consigned anywhere, make a note to check on them every 90 days or so to see if they need more or they need picked up.

If you work with others on your zine, make a box or tray for each person's notes. It helps everyone to stay organized and feel a part of the team. Free apps like Trello and Slack are for creative teams to collaborate on projects and manage all of the moving parts.

Delegating the workload. If you start to receive lots of mail, especially orders, you'll probably need to delegate and organize a system where one person can pick up the work from their teammates so they aren't confused and it doesn't become solely one person's responsibility. Creating a list of duties for each person working on the project is a good idea.

Eliminate anything that is draining your energy and embrace the tasks that you love. Create ways to spend more of your time on the them. Make a list of things that are causing you stress. Are there tasks you can delegate? The sooner you can deal with the bin of mail, the sooner you will clear that space in your head to pay more attention to the things you enjoy. If you ignore anything for too long, it generally ceases to be important.

make your workspace as unique as you are

Back up anything on a computer or in the cloud every month or so. If nothing else, even if these things are never useful again, they can be a really comforting and can be years later. Letters and bad ideas can be a nostalgic reminder of this magical project years after you've forgotten about them and have enough distance to laugh at yourself.

A short filing cabinet (two drawers) makes a great stand for a laser printer, copier, or scanner. It can also be an emergency layout table / mail sorter / bill-paying desk. Create horizontal space in your workspace, do your best to keep it clear, and you will have an easier, more satisfying place to make it happen. If you can live in the city, you can easily find a great free desk on the side of the road. Your desk will stay neater longer if you use small trays or dividers in the drawers. Keep a can filled with pencils, pens, and a letter-opener on your desk. If you haven't used something in six months, throw it away. Every time you handle something, question whether you really need to keep it.

Assembly Area: Unless you're doing everything digitally, you need a large area to assemble your zine, preferably one where you can leave your layout undisturbed as it develops. A used light table comes in handy. A light table with a see-through plastic grid on it allows you to see whether you're pasting objects straight, if you are straight or care about that. You can make your own light table by cutting a sheet of thin white plastic to fit over the top of an aquarium or wooden box with a lamp inside it. Notch the cover in one corner so that you can run the light cord out of the box.

The first issue of *Stink in Public* was hastily written and laid out in one feverishly long night. I am pretty sure that I used every font on my parents' ancient PC, or at least I tried to. Then I pulled whatever magazines, advertisements, and paper out of the trash can and glued the text on top of them. I copied it first thing in the morning and brought it to school the next day, not having slept at all. It is a completely ugly abomination 25 years later but its spirit remains alive and well when old friends still recall its contents and style fondly. If I had never made something so ugly, I never would have made a zine at all or continued to do so. You have to get started somewhere.

Other than the writing, layout and type are the most important elements about making your zine. If it interests you, browse some books on these subjects at the library. Much of this chapter may sound like it only applies to using a computer to produce your zine, but most of the techniques also apply to a handwritten, paste-up, or typewritten style.

Zines come in every size, but the most common in the US are: *half-letter* or *digest,* which is a standard 8-1/2" x 11" sheet folded in half to 5-1/2" x 8-1/2", and *standard,* which is either an 8-1/2" x 11" sheet, unfolded, or an 11" x 17" sheet folded to 8-1/2" x 11". *Quarter* is a half-size cut into two pieces to 5-1/2" x 4-1/4", or to 4-1/4" x 5-1/2". Another size that shows up regularly is *half-legal,* which yields a 7" x 8-1/2" format. European paper sizes differ, but they are rough equivalents to the American ones. Both are shown to the right.

Determine your page orientation and paper size, margin and column sizes, spacing between lines and paragraphs, paragraph alignment (left, right, justified, or mixed), primary typefaces, and perhaps some fun stylistic elements such as ruling lines.

Drawing a rough sketch helps you to determine how much space you can allot to each piece and gives you an idea where to put graphic elements, like photos, ads, line

European paper size chart

Some layout examples. Think of your options besides plain text on a page.

art, and illustrations. Do a sketch for each page. The easiest way to design a page is to take a blank piece of paper and draw your document layout using lines to represent text, as shown above.

Most zines, booklets, and chapbooks are laid out so that each

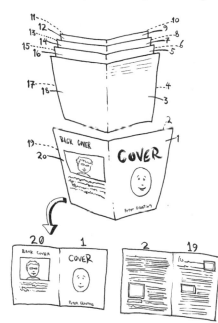

plan your dummy

actual sheet has four pages printed on it. It's easy to see why. Fold a sheet of paper in half. Now number the resulting sides: one, two, three, and four. You have just created a mock-up of a four-page zine. Create your zine in four-page multiples (8, 12, 16, 20, etc), since this is easiest to layout and copy. Unlike books, a zine is expected to have something on every page. You may need to come up with some space-fillers such as jokes, quotes, and illustrations.

Try to finish editing all of your writing before you start layout. It will save you a lot of frustration. One seemingly minor addition or deletion can affect the placement of text for many pages.

Professional designers often use a grid on a computer to draw page layouts. Grids helps you draw even lines and balance your columns.

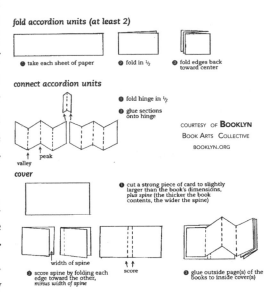

Accordion Book

fold accordion units (at least 2)

❶ take each sheet of paper

❷ fold in ½

❸ fold edges back toward center

connect accordion units

❶ fold hinge in ½

❷ glue sections onto hinge

↑ peak
↑ valley

cover

❶ cut a strong piece of card to slightly larger than the book's dimensions, plus *spine* (the thicker the book contents, the wider the spine)

width of spine

❷ score spine by folding each edge toward the other, minus width of spine

↑ ↑ score

❸ glue outside page(s) of the books to inside cover(s)

COURTESY OF **BOOKLYN** BOOK ARTS COLLECTIVE BOOKLYN.ORG

If you have an illustration or photo that must go on a specific page, place that first, and then build your page around it. You can vary the grid from page to page, but when you're just starting to

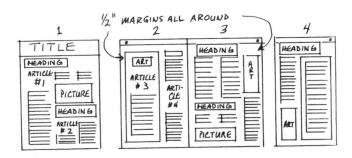

½" MARGINS ALL AROUND

experiment with layout, usually it's better to keep things pretty simple and consistent.

White space is any space on the pages that is blank, such as margins. Effective use of white space tells the eye where to focus. Surrounding an item with white space usually makes it stand out. A dense and cluttered layout is more challenging to read but adds a certain aesthetic appeal. Creative use of white space excites readers.

Try to define page **margin** settings that can serve as the basis for every page in your zine. This simplifies a range of tasks such as folding and stapling. A consistent margin will also appeal to readers.

Try to keep text at least 1/2" away from all four sides of your page. This reduces the risk of cutting off text or images that are close to the edge. You'd think you could just create equal margins all around your page. However, this tends to make the top margin look larger than the sides, and the bottom margin will look small. Instead, start by making the side margins equal, the top margin

DO THIS:

ZINES

Zines are swell and fabulous. We love zines more than life itself. A day without zines is like a day without sunshine. Q: How many zine editors does it take to change a light bulb? A: None, they'll just edit in the dark until someone else can afford to buy the light bulb. Zines are cool, zines are fine, we like zines all the time. Hooray for zines!

NOT THIS:

ZINES

Zines are swell and fabulous. We love zines more than life itself. A day without zines is like a day without sunshine. Q: How many zine editors does it take to change a light bulb? A: None, they'll just edit in the dark until someone else can afford to buy the light bulb. Zines are cool, zines are fine, we like zines all the time. Hooray for zines!

slightly smaller, and the bottom margin larger (up to twice the size of the top).

From there, try a slightly wider margin on the inside of each page to allow plenty of space for stapling or binding. This also makes it easier to read, since the text isn't stuck in the gutter of the fold.

(Paper width) − (column widths + gutter widths) = X

X = total width for left and right margin settings.

a zine can be any size you can think of!

Think of each set of facing pages as a unit rather than as two unrelated parts. Make the margin between the pages about equal to each of the outer margins. Face pages that complement each other and have similar contrast and appearance.

Use at least 1/4" gaps between columns. Otherwise people will read across both columns. Readers grow tired when columns contain fewer than 35 letters or more than 65 letters per line. It's fine to vary the number of columns per page. This is a good way to set off a chart, or to draw focus to a particular item, like an important article. One common effect is to place a picture in the middle of two columns of text, with the text flowing around either side. The picture can be centered between the columns, or off-center.

The best way to learn about **type** is to observe how it is used on the page. Study the newspaper, signs, and labels. You can also use sheets of transfer lettering, rub-on letters, or adhesive lettering. Get it from an art store, drafting supply, or paper store. Find borders clip-art books that you like.

"I Want to Use Every Font!" is a common instinct but just confusing, distracting, and upsetting when you try to read the page. Limit the number of typefaces on a page to two. In fact, it's not a bad idea to limit the number of typefaces in your entire publication to three or four until you become more experienced.

As with any rule, this one has exceptions. On your cover and in ads, use different typefaces to set them apart from the rest of your zine. If you have a number of short pieces, create dramatic effects by using a different font for each heading.

Bold is most often used for headings and emphasis. *Italic* is most often used for titles of publications, such as *The New York Times,* and creative works, such as Mozart's *Requiem* or *Gone With The Wind*. It can also be used for *emphasis;* and finally, this is ***bold italic, which isn't used unless you are making a really emphatic point***.

Body text is usually done in 10-point type because it is very readable. To distinguish headings and captions from body text, vary the point size by at least two points. Thus, 8-point type can be used for captions, and 12-point type for headings. You can vary the style or weight, perhaps using bold for headings and italics for captions.

This is a heading in 12-point bold.

This is body text in 10-point book.

This is a caption in 8-point italic.

Neatly handwritten zines lend an honest, informal quality to a zine that the homeliest typeface can never match. Mixing handwriting and typing can look neat if you do it right. Perhaps handwrite your titles while typing the articles, or vice versa.

- It's hard to make titles and headings too big. You can use a different typeface than the one you choose for body text, like I did in this book. Bold, thick typestyles work well. You can also use white text reversed on a black box (which you can create in Indesign or with the inverse feature on some photocopiers). This will add visual variety right off the bat while helping the reader organize your article, particularly a long one, into more digestible visual pieces.

- There are two basic types of fonts: **Sans and** serif fonts.

- Serif characters have little twigs and loops, which supposedly make the type easier to read at larger sizes while sans fonts are easier to read at small sizes. Sans is commonly used in headers and footers, signs, and pull quotes.

- Avoid widows and orphans (one line of text by itself at the top or bottom of a page respectively). Avoid putting titles at the bottom of a page. Follow headings with at least two lines of text before a page break. If you're using Indesign, you can automate the software to do all of these things, or whatever you want.

- Do not use all uppercase letters for body text, and only in short bursts for titles. It can be difficult to read. All lowercase letters can be distracting but can also create a specific style and feel.

- Learn to use drop caps (an oversize letter, usually a capital) to start articles and section headings like in this book. This is a useful visual variety technique. They look great in pull quotes, too. Indesign automates these too.

- Be careful when wrapping text around an image, as it is nearly impossiblc to follow where to read and disrupts any natural habit that the brain has for reading across the page. Indesign automates this but doesn't have perfect judgment about what looks good or not.

- Consider placing images at the side, top, or bottom of the page or between two text columns to avoid breaking up a line of text.

- Turn off hyphenation unless you're really trying to maximize words on a page.

I'm a strong believer in **justified** text but even so, avoid justifying narrow columns, or you'll run into a lot of problems with weird spacing that l o o k s s t r e t c h e d – o u t.

A pull quote is a popular magazine trick, which involves pulling out an attention-getting or summarizing phrase in an article, and repeating the phrase in enlarged type, spanning it across one or more columns.

Drawing Focus

Blur your sight slightly by narrowing or widening your eyes. Now look at your page. What jumps out? Is it just a wash of gray with no variety? Use this trick throughout the layout stage as a way to check the appearance of your pages. Try it in front of a rack of magazines to improve your cover design too.

Often pull quotes have a *drop cap* (a big capital) as the first letter. Pull quotes serve to draw a reader's attention to a particular point, and they really break up gray space. Place *ruling lines* (horizontal bars above and below the quote) to set it off from the body text. You can also put the pull quote in a box, circle, or any other shape.

Reverse text (white text on a field of gray or black) can be used for pull quotes in the middle of articles, or in corners of pages that need filler material. It is often difficult to read in large quantities, especially if the type size isn't very large. So try to use at least 10-point type, preferably bolded. Avoid typefaces with thin vertical lines (like many serif faces). I find that bold, sans serif type gets the best results since the background's black ink isn't as likely to fill in the letters and clog the type.

Headers & Footers are fixed text at the top or bottom of each page, like in this book. They give a unique feel for zines that are more informational, great works of parody, or to create appeal to people not accustomed to reading zines.

If you're **pasting up** pages by hand, get a waxer or a glue stick. A waxer melts wax strips and applies a thin coating to the back of your original when you roll it across, allowing you the ability to move around the elements after they are attached. A waxer will set you back maybe $50. An $8 box of wax strips seems to last forever. Glue sticks ($1-3) are much cheaper but it's hard to change placement and they don't last very long. Rubber cement and bottled glue are messy, dry lumpy, and ruin your artwork.

Supplies

A transparent ruler is better than an opaque one. Get the most comfortable, flexible scissors you can find ($3 to $10 if you don't already own ones you like.) An X-acto knife is sometimes better than scissors. A paper cutter simplifies and speeds cutting and trimming. Also: a cutting board, Sharpie markers, and scanner. White out is okay until the brush gets lumpy and clogs felt-tip pens. White correction tape is superior.

Be warned: You will discover a typo three minutes before going to the printer. Make peace by fixing it or letting go.

How Do I Do The Cover?

Most new readers will discover a zine because the cover speaks to them, emotionally, graphically, or intellectually. Study some other zines and magazines that you like to see how their covers are composed.

Popular logic is that the title of your zine should occupy the top two inches of your cover. However, sometimes getting out of the box can aid your zine's appearance and uniqueness. Use the largest, widest type possible. It should grab attention.

Most zine covers are black and white, so it immediately makes yours visible to include some color—a colored paper stock, color copies, or spot colors on an offset press are all great choices. Another important thing to include is an image. Shawn Granton of *Ten Foot Rule* makes a sheet of color photocopies to cut up and paste onto the cover of each zine. Sarah of *The Book Bindery* went the opposite route, pasting a black and white photocopy onto the cover of her red-papered cover, which creates a very nice effect as well. Tomas Moniz's *Rad Dad* features limited-edition letterpress covers, giving the zine a really exciting and unique look.

HINT: Use a different color scheme than you used last issue, so that people will immediately visually recognize that it's a new issue. Two issues of *The CIA Makes Science Fiction Unexciting* came out about five years apart with the same red and white color scheme. People still think it's the same issue!

The popularity of color photocopying is also causing prices to drop, as low as 19 cents per page. If you're doing a photocopied zine, you might consider a full color cover.

Put some text on the cover explaining the contents of your zine-–things that you think are exciting about it. Include a list of subjects, contributors, features, interviewees, or any particularly interesting, unusual, or topical stories. If the contents wouldn't be recognizable at a glance, just create a simple and pleasing design instead. Google "*Big Hands* zine by Aaron Smith" for some visually powerful, yet simple cover examples. Creating cover text is a great writing exercise to figure out how to say the most with the fewest number of words possible.

photos, illustration, & pre-press

Like all good zinesters, I've maintained a folder of graphic clippings that accumulated into a filing cabinet and then eventually became thousaznds of scans and photos on my computer. Gradually, I organized these into a system for finding what I need when I need it, even when my memory cannot recall if I have a suitable image or not. I give them names that I would search for later.

You can really improve the emotional impact of your zine with solid images to capture what you want to express. Nowadays, your smart phone has a point-and-shoot digital camera that is more than adequate for printing photos in your zine. There's enough power that you don't need to learn to take pictures, unless, of course, the point of your zine is to showcase photography.

You can find tasteful images, magazines, rubber stamps, and clip art at garage sales, thrift stores, etc. These are also great places to find typewriters, the zinester's best friend. *Crap Hound*[6] is a great zine that features artwork and typefaces taken from a variety of public domain sources that you can reproduce in your zine.

If you can do your own illustration, that's even better, as it will create a unique look and style that people will remember. Look at other zines, for starters, and see whose artwork you like. Perhaps their artist will illustrate for you too, especially if they like what you're doing. I have always found many illustrators and photographers who saw what I was doing and offered to contribute. When you're asking someone to do this, explain your project to them, with contagious enthusiasm. The right people will get excited about your work, and hopefully have some ideas to go with them. Some illustrators are excited to draw pictures from your ideas, while others prefer to come up with the ideas themselves. Make sure that you and your illustrator are on the same wavelength about this.

Collages can be made of appropriated images from other published material, your own photos, or both, although they usually look best when created from similar material (e.g., all glossy magazines, all cut-up photos, or all newsprint images). Be mindful of copyright violations, but don't obsess. In many cases, your use is re-appropriating the intent, meaning, and context of others'

6 *Crap Hound*: $12 from ReadingFrenzy.com

work. Similarly, maybe your use constitutes legal use under the parody clause of fair use. Additionally, your print run is likely not substantial enough to warrant any attention or concern, even if the owner believes that it's illegal.[7] More than anything else, respect your peers! It's one thing to steal photos from a high-end magazine or use expired public domain images, but it is another altogether to use the work of your peers without even asking.

- Group similarly created images together on each two-page spread. Don't mix clip art, a pencil drawing, and a photograph.

- Charts and graphs can illustrate a point effectively or humorously.

- A visual representation of information is often more effective at making your point than the most carefully chosen words. Combining text and graphics hammers it home.

Adobe Photoshop, or its open-source freeware variant Gimp, is the ideal computer program for photo and graphic manipulation. You can import your photos direct from your camera or scanner and resize, edit, or distort them. You can correct contrast and brightness problems as well as convert photos to black and white. As a starting point, I usually turn both the brightness and contrast up 20 points. It may look washed-out on your screen, but you are formatting for paper. Most photocopiers have a photo setting, where you can place a color or black and white photo on the copier, turn on the photo setting, and it'll give you a reproducible copy. You can lighten or darken this print as needed, and what you see is

---

7 For cases when you really need to know for sure, here's a guide to when images enter the public domain. copyright.cornell.edu/resources/publicdomain.cfm

what you get, unlike on a computer screen. When you don't know how to achieve your desired effect, Google it.

Michael T Perkins of *Section 8* zine advises, "Our first 27 issues were cut and paste with glue and scissors. We use to copy them on Xerox machines. Now we do full color to show off the artwork better. Layouts are done with new toys these days, we use Adobe Indesign & Photoshop CS6 (not the creative cloud shit)." Matthew Thompson offers, "I plan to learn InDesign, which is how *Fluke #13* was laid out. I am really happy with the results and sometimes laugh at myself for not doing it that way up until 2016."

If you are importing or scanning photos for your zine, you'll want to have your final images at least 300 dots-per-inch (DPI) and at the final print size. DPI is exactly what it says, the number of dots per inch that are used to create a composite image to the eye. You can't enlarge digital photos without a rapid loss in quality.

An older copier reproduces and muddies gray photos into something dark and indecipherable. A **halftone** *is an image setting, most commonly used for photos, where a field of intermittent tiny black dots are used to resemble gray*, like you see in newspaper photos. Keith Rosson and Aaron Cometbus use blown up halftone patterns to great effect as an aesthetic design. You can create a similar effect on a photocopier by repeatedly enlarging and rotating your image until it appears as a dot pattern.

To create a halftone in Gimp or Photoshop, pull down the "image" menu, select "mode," and choose "bitmap." If bitmap is not an option, first chose "grayscale" and then go back and choose "bitmap." One of your bitmap options is "halftone screen." Choose that and it'll prompt your output resolution and dot pattern. Typically, a "round" dot pattern at 100-150 line screen looks best but you can Google or ask your copy shop or printer.

HINT: If your prints come back too dark, turn down the image brightness on the copier or adjust the image in Photoshop or try a line screen of 85. Photos with high contrast tend to look best.

If you "layout directly onto the page and use a lot of white out, cavewoman style," like Ayun Halliday of *East Village Inky,* then the pasted up pages are your master. Sometimes it makes sense to scan these and create a digital file so that the originals don't degrade or get destroyed through trips to the copy shop. Most copy shops or print shops prefer being sent a PDF file that they can print directly from your email through their digital printing equipment.

If you print in full color, convert your pages in Photoshop or Gimp by going to "Image", "Mode", "CMYK." This converts screen colors (RGB) to print colors so the colors look correct on the page.

But for real artistic flair, adding blockprinting or screenprinting to your zine makes it look and feel very interesting and warm. And it's super easy to do either!

BLOCK PRINTING
instructions

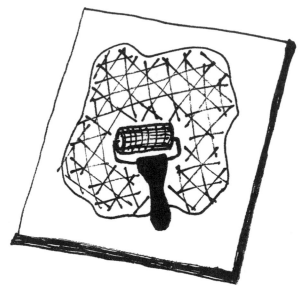

Blockprinting is a very simple way to add texture and color to your zine pages—particularly your covers! It takes a little more time and love than photocopying, but it's something special. Here are simple instructions, created by Eleanor Whitney for the Portland Zine Symposium, for adding blockprinting to your zine!

Learning to Block Print............

1. Obtain a slab of lineoleum, rubber, or like material. Obtain "cutting tools." These items are readily available at art stores.

2. Using a pencil, draw your design onto a slab of material. Then, use cutting tools (safety first!) to cut out either the marks you made w/ your pencil <u>or</u> the surrounding areas. The areas you <u>don't</u> cut are the ones that will print. Therefore, if you want a positive of your image, cut out the surrounding area of your pencil marks. If you want a negative of your image, cut out your pencil marks. Different types of cutting tools achieve various sorts of cuts. Test out your tools & skills on extra slabs of material before you cut into your drawing.

3. Inking your block up cleanly & smoothly might take a bit of practice. Recommended ink for use is water soluable kinds because these lend well for clean-up & don't emit harmful fumes. Obtain a small (8x8 inches, for example) piece of plexiglass & squirt about two teaspoons of your ink of choice on it. Obtain a small rubber roller (also available at art stores) and evenly distribute ink onto plexi with it. "Evenly distribute" = ink should be spread thin all over plexi & the rubber roller's interaction w/ ink & plexi will create an unmistakeable "ch-ch-ch" sound.

4. Now, take your roller fully loaded w/ it's smooth layer of ink & apply it evenly to the surface of your lineoleum, rubber, or block material.

material.

5. Place the paper / cardstock / whatever you are printing onto over the inked block & don't move it! (Smears ruin designs.) Press hard onto paper with a wooden spoon or brayer (art store item) until you think that our design has successfully transferred onto your surface.

5. Carefully lift up a corner to check if your design really has transferred. If it has not, put corner back down without moving anything, & continue pressing & rubbing. If it has successfully transferred lift your surface (paper, etc.) off the block surface in one full, careful swoop!

6. Put your print in a safe place to dry. Repeat steps 4 & 5 until you have your desired # of prints. You will have to keep adding ink in small amounts to plexi w/ roller in order to keep you ink on roller fresh & flowing.

7. Clean-up! If you used water-soluable ink you can wash your block carving with warm, soapy water & blot dry. If you used oil-based ink, use turpentine / mineral spirits & paper towel to rub surface clean. (And dispose of your flammable paper towels!)

8. Congratulations! You are a block printer!

SCREEN PRINTING

JOHN ISAACSON

NO MONEY? NO JOB? NO CONNECTIONS? NO ELECTRICITY?
SCREEN PRINTING CAN BE EASY IF YOU HAVE TONS OF
PATIENCE, PERSEVERANCE, AND LOVE IN YOUR HEART.

→ POSSIBILITIES ←

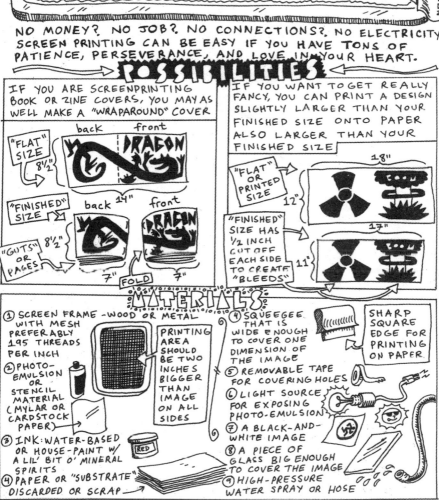

IF YOU ARE SCREENPRINTING BOOK OR ZINE COVERS, YOU MAY AS WELL MAKE A "WRAPAROUND" COVER

"FLAT" SIZE 8½"

back   front
DRAGON

"FINISHED" SIZE

back 14" front DRAGON

"GUTS" OR PAGES 8½"

7" FOLD 7"

IF YOU WANT TO GET REALLY FANCY, YOU CAN PRINT A DESIGN SLIGHTLY LARGER THAN YOUR FINISHED SIZE ONTO PAPER ALSO LARGER THAN YOUR FINISHED SIZE

"FLAT" OR PRINTED SIZE 12"   18"   BOOM

"FINISHED" SIZE HAS ½ INCH CUT OFF EACH SIDE TO CREATE "BLEEDS"   11"   17"   BOOM

MATERIALS

① SCREEN FRAME - WOOD OR METAL WITH MESH PREFERABLY 195 THREADS PER INCH

② PHOTO-EMULSION OR STENCIL MATERIAL (MYLAR OR CARDSTOCK PAPER)

③ INK: WATER-BASED OR HOUSE-PAINT W/ A LIL' BIT O' MINERAL SPIRITS

④ PAPER OR "SUBSTRATE" DISCARDED OR SCRAP

RED

PRINTING AREA SHOULD BE TWO INCHES BIGGER THAN IMAGE ON ALL SIDES

④ SQUEEGEE THAT IS WIDE ENOUGH TO COVER ONE DIMENSION OF THE IMAGE

⑤ REMOVABLE TAPE FOR COVERING HOLES

⑥ LIGHT SOURCE FOR EXPOSING PHOTO-EMULSION

⑦ A BLACK-AND-WHITE IMAGE

⑧ A PIECE OF GLASS BIG ENOUGH TO COVER THE IMAGE

⑨ HIGH-PRESSURE WATER SPRAY OR HOSE

SHARP SQUARE EDGE FOR PRINTING ON PAPER

DESIGNING AN IMAGE

THE SIMPLICITY OF YOUR PRINT IS ALMOST DIRECTLY PROPORTIONAL TO THE NUMBER OF COLORS IN IT.

OVER THROW THE GOVERNMENT
TOMORROW PEOPLE'S PARK

1 COLOR

FASHION SHOW

2 COLORS - NON-REGISTERING

BAD DUDES

3-COLORS - TIGHT REGISTRATION

EASY → MODERATE → DIFFICULT

IF YOU ARE USING WATER-BASED INKS, YOU CAN CREATE ADDITIONAL COLORS BY OVERLAPPING COLORS

TWO COLOR PRINT

CREATES THREE COLORS

BLUE

YELLOW

GREEN MADE BY OVERLAPPING YELLOW AND BLUE

YOU MUST SEPARATE THE COLORS BY HAND OR DIGITALLY ON A COMPUTER. PRINT OR DRAW EACH COLOR ON A SEPARATE TRANSPARENT SHEET

C A Y

R Z

BLUE

YELLOW

REGISTRATION MARKS HELP TO LINE UP THE COLORS WITH EACH OTHER ... + ⊕

EACH IMAGE MUST BE PRINTED OUT IN BLACK IN ORDER TO BLOCK-OUT LIGHT WHEN THE SCREEN IS EXPOSED.

LIGHT
SCREEN
GLASS
IMAGE

PHOTO EMULSION

DESIGNING AN IMAGE WITH NO COLORS THAT TOUCH EACH OTHER WILL SAVE YOU THE STRESS OF TIGHT, EXACT COLOR REGISTRATION

THE CRAZY SAILORS PLAYING AT THE BOTTOM OF THE SHOE
11/17 8PM $4.00

PRETEND THIS IMAGE IS BLUE

PRETEND THIS TEXT IS RED

VISUALIZE THIS "PAPER" AS A CREAMY OFF-WHITE

REMEMBER YOU CAN USE THE PAPER AS ANOTHER COLORFUL ELEMENT IN YOUR DESIGN.

STENCIL

PRINT

PAPER COLOR

PRINTING

YET ANOTHER ITEM YOU MAY NEED FOR PRINTING ARE THE AMAZING "JIFFY CLAMPS" THAT HOLD THE SCREEN IN PLACE, YET ALSO LET YOU RAISE & LOWER THE SCREEN

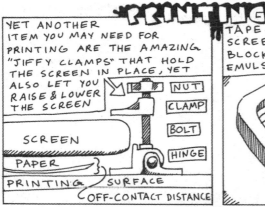

NUT
CLAMP
BOLT
HINGE

SCREEN
PAPER
PRINTING SURFACE
OFF-CONTACT DISTANCE

TAPE-OUT ANY AREAS OF SCREEN THAT ARE NOT BLOCKED BY EMULSION

TAPE SOME TRACING PAPER OR CLEAR FILM UNDER THE PRINTING SURFACE UNDER THE SCREEN

SCREEN
JIFFY CLAMPS, AMAZING!
TAPE, AGAIN
CLEAR FILM

LIL' PIECE OF CARDBOARD FOR OFF CONTACT

FLOOD THE IMAGE BY COVERING IT WITH INK. NOW YOU ARE PRIMED TO PRINT!

INK

TO PRINT, START AT THE TOP OF THE SCREEN, AWAY FROM WHERE YOU STAND. HOLD THE SQUEEGEE AT A 45-60 DEGREE ANGLE, PUSH DOWN **HARD** WHILE PULLING THE SQUEEGEE TOWARDS YOU.

YOU MAY HAVE TO PULL THE SQUEEGEE 2-3 TIMES ACROSS

OFF CONTACT DISTANCE CLOSED

LIFT THE SCREEN UP AND SLIDE YOUR PAPER UNDER THE TRANSPARENT SHEET YOU JUST PRINTED ON.

PAPER

NAIL + PIECE OF WOOD = KICK STAND

PRINT ON
CLEAR FILM

EXPOSING THE IMAGE

POUR A BEAD OF EMULSION* ON THE SCREEN:

"TEXTURE"

EMULSION

"POURING"

BUCKET

"BEAD"

* MANY TYPES OF EMULSION MUST BE MIXED WITH A SENSITIZER FIRST!

USING A STRAIGHT-EDGE OR PIECE OF CARDBOARD, SCRAPE THE EMULSION EVENLY ON TO THE SCREEN

A THIN COAT WORKS BEST

YOUTH OF TODAY

EMULSION

ALSO WORKS

COAT IN BOTH DIRECTIONS ON BOTH SIDES

LET IT DRY OVERNIGHT IN THE <u>DARK</u>. EXPOSING THE SCREEN TO LIGHT WILL MAKE THE EMULSION HARDEN AND BECOME WATER PROOF = MAGICAL POWERS

BOTTOM OF SCREEN

DARKNESS

LIL' BLOCKS

SET UP YOUR EXPOSURE SYSTEM. THE VARIABLES ARE WATTAGE, SCREEN SIZE, DISTANCE BETWEEN LIGHT SOURCE AND SCREEN, AND DURATION OF EXPOSURE

ULTRA VIOLET LIGHT

EXPOSURE TIME ≈ TWO MINUTES

250 WATT BULB

EXPOSURE TIME ≈ TEN SECONDS

SCREEN BOOK

HOT TIP: USE A PIECE OF GLASS TO KEEP IMAGE IN CONTACT WITH THE SCREEN

LIGHT

GAY

#LVE

WET TIP: WASH SCREEN OUT <u>IMMEDIATELY</u> AFTER EXPOSURE

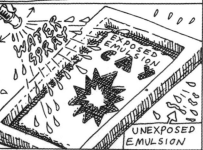

WATER SPRAY

EXPOSED EMULSION

GAY

UNEXPOSED EMULSION

WHEN YOU HAVE YOUR PAPER POSITIONED WHERE YOU WANT IT, USE TAPE TO MAKE REGISTRATION MARKS WHERE THE CORNERS OF THE PAPER WILL FIT. FOLDING THE PAPER TO SIZE CAN HELP FOR POSITIONING

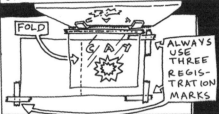

ALWAYS USE THREE REGISTRATION MARKS

ONCE THE REGISTRATION MARKS ARE IN PLACE ON YOUR PRINTING SURFACE, YOU ARE READY TO BEGIN YOUR PRINT RUN. REMOVE THE CLEAR FILM

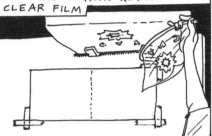

IT'S NICE TO HAVE A FRIEND WHO CAN HELP YOU PRINT.

BLAH BLAH

BLAH

MUSIC HELPS TOO →

WHEN YOU ARE DONE PRINTING THE FIRST OR "BOTTOM" COLOR, USE WATER TO CLEAN THE INK OFF YOUR FIRST SCREEN AND PUT THE SCREEN THAT HAS THE IMAGE FOR YOUR SECOND COLOR INTO THE CLAMPS

LATER DUDE!

YOU WILL HAVE TO MAKE NEW REGISTRATION MARKS TO LINE UP YOUR PRINTS OF THE FIRST COLOR TO THE SCREEN OF THE SECOND COLOR

TIP: YOU CAN SEE THRU THE SCREEN BEFORE YOU PUT INK ON IT

THIS CAN HELP YOU REGISTER COLORS

MAKE LITTLE ADJUSTMENTS TO WHERE YOU PLACE THE PAPER IF YOU NEED. DON'T PANIC! PERFECTIONISM CRIPPLES CREATIVITY!

THESE AREN'T QUITE STRAIGHT...

I MAKE THEM CROOKED ON PURPOSE

IT'S JUST MY "STYLE"

CRAZY

WHATEVER, DUDE

paper, printing, binding

O nce upon a time, *Stink in Public* was printed by a guy in a cool band who worked at a copy shop in Kent, about 40 miles from my parent's house. He didn't send me a bill for the printing and I could either drive over there or pay to ship them. It was a godsend until he got bored with grand theft photocopy and left the job. Then I realized how much I took it for granted. Naturally, many other free options surfaced quickly in my underworld network. Not everyone goes this route, of course, and you can often tell immediately by the subject matter in the zines. Sometimes people will tell you their secrets in a letter when they wouldn't print it in their zine, such as how they print their zine.

Nowadays, I use a photocopy store in the neighborhood. I email them files and quantities and they deliver boxes of printed, folded, and stapled zines. You can probably find something comparable where you live. It makes the most sense to do photocopying locally, unless you have a totally free hookup somewhere else. "The *East Village Inky* has been printed by Wholesale Copies on 28th and 5th Avenue in NYC since issue #2. Tell 'em the Inky sent you!" says Ayun Halliday. Michael T Perkins of *Section 8* zine takes it one step further, "Buy a used copy machine, and don't be scared to ask for money to make more zines. We've always been on a shoestring budget but if we were more business-minded in the beginning our shoelaces would be "fat laces." Most zines don't provide fat laces to their editors but are simply stapled twice through all of the pages along the fold. A saddle stapler staples on the spine after you've already folded your zine. A long arm staples before you've folded it in half. Either one has limits: 10-15 sheets of paper (40-60 pages).

Andalusia of the radical women's bicycle zine *Clitical Mass* prints her zines entirely on the back of already printed paper that is truly 100% post consumer, instead of recycling it. This requires a lot of found paper but is a great way to lower the global impact of your publishing.

Modern copiers can do folding and stapling just by programming the machine to do so. I think we pay several cents per staple and after having

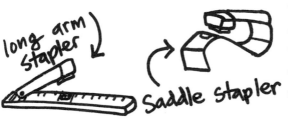

done it myself for twenty years, my wrist is thankful. Folding and stapling 500 zines could reasonably take about 16-20 hours of your time. You may find that part of the job joyous or laborious. Act accordingly!

HINT: You can see if a copy shop has an electric saddle stapler. Maybe you can use it; but it helps to make some copies first, and then hit them up for the stapler. The electric saddle staplers have a foot switch that pulls staples from a spool of wire—simple and easy. If they don't have an electric saddle stapler, they probably have a manual stapler you can use.

Aside from stapling, there are other options to consider. If you want your zine to sit flat when it's open—good for cook zines or how-to manuals—look into comb and wire spiral binding at your copy shop or office supply store.

Any kind of paper-fastening system could work for a zine. How about using a three-prong folder as a cover? They come in colors, and you could paste a color-photocopy inset onto the cover. Round metal brads, safety pins, and sewing are other possibilities. I've seen zines bound with string or rubber bands, but the latter is a bad idea as they become brittle and break.

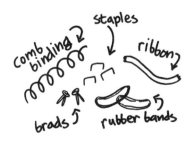

Christoph Meyer of *28 Pages Lovingly Bound with Twine* was the king of binders, because, as you might imagine, he really did hand-tie each copy three times with pieces of twine. The exception to this was the dental issue, which was bound with dental floss. Being creative like this is what is so empowering about zines. You have a wealth of options.

Collating is the process of putting the pages in order. Make sure your photocopier is set to do this automatically as well as printing on both sides of the page (called "double sided") before you start copying. This will save many hours of work.

If your zine is very thick, then you can give it a hot look by **trimming** it along the vertical edge. When you fold a lot of sheets, the outside sheets are going to be stick out less than the inside sheets, like how runners are staggered in a race. You can do it with a paper cutter or pay your print to do it.

Printing

Once upon a time indie rock boys polluted the Earth with vast stacks of newsprint zines that had little of substance to say and left our fingers as black as their hearts. The nostalgic trauma of revisiting this format should be enough reason not to impose it on your readers even if the dirty fingers aren't.

Chris Boarts Larson, creator of now-defunct punk zine *Slug & Lettuce* explained her thought process to me. "I printed 1,000 copies of a four-sheet tabloid paper for about $150. It increased in pages and copies in increments till I reached 10,000 copies and 20 pages. I capped myself at that to keep it under two ounces to mail. I made the type smaller and smaller to continue to fit more and more into the pages, while keeping it free, something which was essential. I would have loved to have used a nicer grade of paper which for one thing would have held the tones for the photographs much better, and also would have been cleaner on the hands reading it, but it was not an option."

Justin, former coordinator of *Maximum Rocknroll,* explained the math that he had to manage thusly "Our monthly print run was 5,000 copies, which costs about $5,500 a month. We give 265 copies each month to columnists, advertisers, former/current shitworkers, and organizations we support. We send 2,500 to our main distributor and the remainder are either sent to smaller punk distros/stores."

Jackson Ellis, publisher of the music zine *Verbicide,* explained his own decisions, *"Verbicide* is free. We circulate it in as many cities and venues as we can afford. 25,000 copies is my benchmark and I could *easily* distribute 50,000 copies but couldn't sell enough advertising to pay for it." Todd Taylor, editor of *Razorcake,* faced related decisions, "The first issue had a newsprint cover. Too many of them were damaged in the mail, so we went with a glossy cover. We went to bright newsprint three years back because I like seeing clearer photos in print." At *Maximum Rocknroll,* Justin inherted a legacy decision, "The magazine's founder, Tim Yohannan, felt that a newsprint punk zine could never sell out, and it's one of the rules he established at the magazine before he passed away." Jackson got to make his own decisions but recognized that production upgrades aren't always for the best, "I used to be obsessed with the notion of going glossy someday. It seemed like that was the thing to do, the way to succeed, and I was jealous of zines that jumped to glossy but now those magazines are out of business."

Unless your dreams are grandiose and your reality supports them, it makes the most sense to begin by photocopying. 100-200 copies is a good starting place. You can print as many or as few copies as you want and it's easy to make more when you run out. You don't need to save up money for a print run and you get instant gratification.

Once you're making 1,000 copies of your zine at a time, offset makes more sense than photocopying. Offset printing is a lithographic process, meaning that ink and water are run through cylinders and cling to the parts of the paper where the press indicates. Films are used to create plates from your artwork and it takes more time to set up the press than it does to print the zines. You'll find that beyond 1,000 copies, you are really just paying for the cost of paper and the person's time.

Some good offset printers are:

1984Printing.com (Oakland, CA)

ParcellPress.com (Richmond, VA)

EberhardtPress.org (Portland, OR)

Kansas City Book Manufacturing (Kansas City, MO)

UGLLC.net (Matoon, IL, for 3,000+ copies)

Tell 'em that Joe from Microcosm sent ya. All four are familiar with zines and the kinds of questions you will have. You'd be amazed that the printer down the street can cost ten times as much because they don't have the right equipment for your zine or just don't want the job.

There are three main factors of printing—(1) print quality, (2) turnaround time, (3) cost. Common wisdom dictates that no printer can provide all three, but this is false. It can be done! You must also consider how pleasant it is to deal with your printer. This can be a total deal breaker.

When you have a question, don't be afraid to ask. It's your money, and you're paying the printer to guide you. United Graphics once told me that if we made our page .25" narrower, we could save $800 per job! Your printer should have a guide for preparing photos and you should follow it. Get to know everyone's formats and their flexibilities.

Be friendly from the get-go. This will be more valuable than you can dream of. They'll be more likely to cut you slack on the price and payments. Don't break agreements or bring them unfinished work that requires extra coddling on their part. Communicate clearly about what you need and when you need it. Get samples of the paper stock and some of their finished print work.

On rare occasion, a printer will refuse to print your material because they find the content objectionable. You can prevent this by asking if they would have a problem printing something outrageous, such as obscene words or something incendiary or politically radical. Think of the most obscene graphic image you would ever consider publishing, and ask if it would be a problem. It's better to find out up front than after you submit your job.

New Leaf is a paper company that uses 100% post-consumer recycled paper (rather than just recycling paper off the print shop floor). Ask your printer what 100% PCW papers they have in stock. There are other kinds of completely tree-free paper like Kenaf that you may want to investigate as well.

To get an offset price quote, email your printer with your specifications: number of pages, finished size (width x height), type of paper, type of cover and binding you want, and the number of copies you want, number of colors on the cover, special effects (such as varnishes or gatefold covers), and where you want them shipped. Ask how long it takes.

Printing your zine offset creates a new and infinite set of possibilities. You can use different colors of ink, inserts that do not conform to the zine's size, heavier paper for the cover with various coatings, and *Pantone color*. Pantone Matching System (PMS) is a color matching system that assigns a number to every shade of a color, enabling you to specify very precise colors to your printer, in a universal language. Think of a pantone like a paint sample. Start with it as a second color on the cover.

If you have glued pockets or other complicated assembly aspects of your zine you will likely have to do these yourself.

HINT: If you like the print job on a particular zine, find out who their printer is. Ask them what the paper is called. If they're no longer using that printer, find out why.

HINT: Find out if you have to pay for extras ("overs") if the printer prints too many.

Cometbus uses large scale offset printing without adopting the visual trappings of a magazine. Around 12,000 copies of each issue are printed on white paper, and the result is a nicely edited, trimmed, and typeset black-and-white zine.

Most full color work is printed in the third world—Hong Kong, Singapore, or China—because the labor to set up the machine is so expensive that shipping them across the globe on forced child labor is cheaper. Still, it's probably outside of your budget (and ethics).

HINT: Pantones often look very different on screen than they do on paper. Get samples.

HINT: If you are printing red, you can get pink for free by making those areas of red only 10% color. This can work especially well with background colors, where this pastel effect is common.

Always do what is best for your zine rather than your ego.

binding your zines into a book, an at-home guide

① SUPPLIES

sew or staple your zines like you would normally.

find a glue gun and some glue

Optional: get a jigsaw or x-acto if you want your image to extend off the page (and don't fear power tools)

② THE FRAME

Get some 2x4" that are the length of your finished book and glue or screw them into a piece of plywood with the gap between them being the width of your book's spine.

③ THE COVER

Design your cover so the spine fits snugly around all of your interior pages. If you want the image to extend off the page, add an extra .25" all the way around the edge as shown.

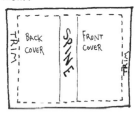

TRIM | BACK COVER | SPINE | FRONT COVER | TRIM

④ ASSEMBLY

Fold and insert your cover into your frame and add liberal amounts of glue onto the inside of the spine.

6 CUTTING
(Optional)

Cut the excess off of all three sides, edge to edge. Don't hurt yourself.

5 BINDERY

Force the interior pages into the glue, slide them back and forth, and hold them there for a few seconds. As the glue dries, remove any excess.

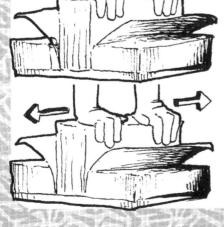

7 GIVE TO FRIENDS

Early and often.

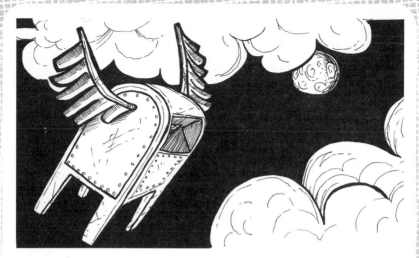

postage

In 2001 I was standing in line at the Post Office with my friend Matthew. He began thumbing through my packages of zines, "Iceland, suburbs of Chicago, Australia, suburbs of Chicago, United Kingdom...Damn Joe, you're an international man of mystery!" The fact that this impressed him was especially meaningful because his grandmother was one of the bestselling true crime authors of all time. It's easy to forget how magical it is to send your work all over the planet. The mail system offers a cheap way to do that.

Nurture a positive relationship with your postal workers! This will help more than you can imagine in a year or two. It's a good bet that your post-person will be a lot more understanding when problems arise if you've taken the time to develop a personal relationship.

The post office has created flat-rate volume-based **Priority Mail** envelopes and boxes. This is to your advantage since they can contain a lot of zines, are relatively cheap, and normally arrive in two to three days.[1]

Media mail must contain "books," which are defined as "8 or more pages bound together, that do not contain advertisements." If your package weighs more than seven ounces, it's cheaper to send it via media mail. You pay a flat fee for the first pound, and subsequent pounds are cheaper. This is an efficient and cheap way to send copies of your zine to a store or distributor. The Postal Service will sometimes refuse to let you use Media Mail to send zines, but the distinction between a "pamphlet" and a "book" is mostly arbitrary. Your best defense is to know the fine print, "But ma'am, this is a book over 8 pages, bound, with no paid advertising. It contains no correspondence."

The cheapest **International Mail**[2] options are the same flat rate envelopes and boxes as with Priority Mail, unless you are mailing something 5 ounces or less. You'll need to fill out a little green customs form including what is inside your package and the value. Zines are described as pamphlets so people know what the hell you're talking about. The United Kingdom and Canada both have pretty fierce taxes on imported paper, so it's often best to keep the stated value per package as low as possible.

And remember, to get the best mail you first have to send the best mail!

---

1 usps.com/ship/mail-shipping-services.htm
2 usps.com/international/mail-shipping-services.htm

Sales

distribution

Like Aaron Cometbus before me, I started to travel the country in 1998, going door-to-door to stores with a box of my zines. Before long this turned into an elaborate mail order network and by 2005, Microcosm had accidentally become the largest distributor of zines in the world. Of course, that wasn't very hard because there wasn't anyone else trying. There is so little money in zines that other motivations must again be your prevailing drive to succeed. And distribution is often the side of things that most people ignore.

Start locally. Figure out some stores that would logically sell your zines. You can tell people that you meet to find and buy them there. Bookstores and record stores are obvious choices but if your zine is about cats, sell it at the pet store. If it's about coffee, sell it at local cafés. Try the cool comic shops, clothing shops, piercing parlors, DIY boutiques, infoshops, beauty parlors, and candy shops. One local bar even has a vending machine with zines in it. Ask people you know who do zines in your area and they can direct you to some stores. There's even specialty zine shops.[3] Figure out the places in your town that *should* be selling zines. Stores that don't presently sell zines are the best place to sell yours, as it will be the most visible one—probably placed on the counter!

Figure out how to describe your zine's ethos and content in five seconds. If it tells a good story, or if it makes people laugh, that's a *big* plus. Drop by a few times and be friendly and chatty. Often times they'll pick it up on the spot. Come back if they aren't yet interested. Most stores will take somewhere between 2 and 20 copies of your zine at a time. A common number to start out with is 5, in order to judge how fast they will sell.

Don't price your zine too high. Try to keep it $2-5 in stores. Look at other zines with similar production and see what they're charging. Your audience may be a factor as well. Readers of a zine on California wines probably have more to spend than flea market fans. A once-obscure, now-popular zine could raise its cover price...and drop it again, depending on the popularity and whims of each following issue. Increasing page count, a screen-printed cover, labor-intensive packaging, adding color, or other obvious improvements justify a higher price to the reader. Of course, it's a good idea to correlate your cover price to what it costs you to make each copy.

---

3 http://www.brokenpencil.com/retail-outlets

Todd Taylor of *Razorcake* looks at his whole budget, "Printing: $2,800, Boxes, tape, labels: $300, Postage: $2,000. We have a comprehensive protocol so we don't over-run or under-run the zine. We have a subscriber base of 1,000 and send 3,500 copies for distribution. We constantly have to update the database. We have 100 copies of each issue left for new subscribers and orders."

A store will generally want 40% of the cover price of your zine. That means you'll get 60%. Price your zine accordingly before you talk to the store and know your numbers.

Each time you sell zines, make an invoice. Include all of your contact information, the date, quantities, titles, wholesale price, and totals. It makes things easier for the people writing you checks if you give them a clear and readable invoice with all of your information. Keep a copy for yourself too. *Put it in safe place. Now.*

To sell your zine through a store in a different city, send them a single copy for free with your email address and a note requesting that they consider selling it. If you don't hear back, follow up after two weeks.

Once a store has your zines, check up on how they are selling every 90 days and be patient. Most importantly, support the stores that sell your zines! Look at what else they sell. Odds are they have other things you'd be interested in besides your zine.

Sometimes they call to say they're sold out and want more copies of the current issue. Sometimes they double their previous order. Sometimes they say how much they like your zine. Sometimes buyers become your friends.

Stores are like people. Each has its own personality and way of doing things. Like people, stores are sometimes inconsistent. And, as with people, you will like some stores more than others. The good ones are supportive and professional (and probably read your zine!), while some are appalling in their utter lack of care or competence. Do what makes you feel good. Always.

One clerk or buyer may be the sole "anchor" for zines at a particular store; if she goes, that may spell the end of the store's zine-friendly attitude. Similarly, DIY zine distributors ("distros") come and go at an alarming rate. Investigate who has quit since your last issue.

HINT: If you're freaked out about making calls, set a time limit. Don't stop making calls until the time is up.

Consignment

Many stores won't pay for zines until they've sold. The money that a store makes from selling zines barely makes it worthwhile for the amount of time and paperwork required to price, display, and collect money for them. Stores that sell zines generally do so because they *want* to and care about the concept and content.

Whether you want to do consignment with stores is up to you. Sometimes, it can work best when sending zines out of town on consignment, to think of them as a donation. Sometimes the time spent trying to collect a few dollars can outweigh the time, effort, and stress of succeeding. Remember, the greatest joy is getting feedback from people reading your zine in those towns!

Don't be disappointed if your first issue doesn't sell like hotcakes, or even your second. But if you're still not selling after the third try, then ponder if it's the right place for your zine, right price for your zine, and how else you might reach your audience.

HINT: Cash is better than consignment because it reduces everyone's paperwork.

Distributors

In almost every quiet suburb there's a zine nerd secretly operating a mail order distro out of their parent's house.[4] These are great places to find thematic zines on various subjects or to have someone else vet the quality of what you are putting your time into. They are also a great way to read different readers with your zine. Just like stores, distros are run by individuals who are just high on zines. Many do zines themselves that you should order and read. Sometimes a distro will have a local presence, at punk shows, comic shows, or sold in local stores. Most have a cool focus and good taste. "Sticky Institute was an absolutely wonderful introduction to the world of distros. They accept everything, their paperwork is simple, and it's absolutely clear what happens in

---

4 http://zinewiki.com/List_of_Distros

regards to what happens if you sell, sell out, don't sell and the timeframe involved." Jaime Nyx of SeaGreenZines.com told me.

There are also larger, wholesale distributors, though they are increasingly antiquated. "We worked with two large independent distributors. Both went out of business, owing people a lot of money, and taking many independent publications down with them. Selling through traditional distributors ends up with 70% of the copies going into the trash. I'd rather give them away." Jackson Ellis of *Verbicide* told me. Dan Sinker from *Punk Planet* once quipped, that, instead of sending his zine to distributors, he would have saved a lot of money and trouble if he'd just loaded the thousands of copies immediately into a dumpster.

Justin, formerly of *Maximum Rocknroll* told me, "As our distributor shifted from being an independent music distributor to working with major-label-controlled music distribution networks, we left for ethical reasons. Our plan now is handle distribution ourselves." Still, distributors remain, like AK Press, Microcosm Publishing, and Pioneers Press, that have websites and mail-order catalogs and sell to individuals as well as stores. They pay 40% of the cover price and can get your zine into more stores than you would probably care to spend the time on yourself.

While it is often not practical for a store to order copies of a single zine, try working together with some friends to create your own distribution co-op of zines, making it practical for stores to order a cluster of zines together. Synchronize your publishing schedules. Share responsibilities for soliciting orders and shipping copies. This makes it much easier for stores to stock the various zines.

ILLUSTRATION BY JULIA WERTZ • 2008 • WWW.FARTPARTY.ORG

getting the word out

In 1997 my zine was reviewed in *Factsheet Five,* which touted a circulation of 16,000 copies. Even though the review was not particularly glowing and rather downright mediocre, I got hundreds of orders and began exchanging letters with many people who I'm still in touch with today. I began sending out catalogs for Microcosm with my zine, which created a path of circular interest over the coming years. I designed and printed 5,000 4x6" postcards for $99 and rather than using one side for mailing, I designed both sides to talk about Microcosm, what we stand for, and the kind of zines that we have. Suddenly I had people to mail them to, who I could ask to mail them to their friends, in turn.

It worked. Before long the word of mouth had spread and I was receiving orders from names and cities that I didn't recognize. Microcosm established a critical mass and had gone viral by 2001 and people who ordered were likely to order again.

Similarly, I traded ads with other zines and printed them in my zine. Doing so is free and it's mutual aid. Most zines could use more graphic images anyway, and ads help you to meet and relate with other zinesters. When you have questions or a problem, you have someone that you can talk to about it.

Mike Rodemann created an ad for his zine *9 1/2 Left* (a reference to losing part of a finger as a child) which simply featured a photo of a man holding a large fish pasted up with his address, the price, and the name of his zine. While it indicated nothing about his zine, it's an enticing picture that somehow works as an ad.

From there, the world is your oyster. "People give the *East Village Inky* as baby shower gifts," says Ayun Halliday. "We leave zines on the shelves of our sponsors and at the public library," Michael T Perkins of *Section 8* offered. "Corbett Redford passed a copy of *Fluke* to Iggy Pop. Iggy Pop has an issue of *Fluke*. What more could I ask for?" Matthew Thompson told me.

To keep up momentum, you just have to keep people interested and engaged, which shouldn't be too hard if you are relatively consistent in terms of what you are yakking about and how often. Start a mailing list of the people who have ordered your zine and let them know what you're up to and when. Create social media accounts and post about not only your zine but things of related interest.

Reviews

Reviews and word-of-mouth recommendations are probably the best promotion you can get for your zine. Send every issue to *Xerography Debt, Razorcake, Maximumrocknroll, Zine Thug,* among others.[5] Blogs and magazines that are thematically similar to your zine will often review it, even if they don't typically review zines.

Zine readings and similar events can be very successful for putting your zine in front of new audiences. Put up flyers around town, send out press releases to your local papers, and be an actively engaged participant on forums where you talk about more than just your zine. Similarly, *Maximum Rocknroll* is very open to interview submissions) just like podcasts like to feature anyone who is an engaged member of their subculture. There are also online fan groups covering everyone from Madonna to Noam Chomsky and your zine inevitably fits into some of these niche forums.

Making stickers for your zine and putting them where others will see them costs about $20 and you can send some to other zines and readers to put up.

Zine librarians tend to talk up things that they like as well so send them copies of your zine.

"Small business owners, concert promoters and DJs, art galleries, art supply stores, and weed shops need us and are happy to pay for advertising. When we were younger we felt that selling ads was selling out. But know we just focus on making as many beautiful zines for our readers that we can." Michael of *Section 8* offered.

5 https://brooklyncollegezines.commons.gc.cuny.edu/zine-resources/

• Offer subscriptions online or through the post office.

• Create a blog / website / social media page

• Post photos of your zine

• Get recommended and linked on fan sites.

• A new way to promote your work comes into existence every five minutes.

Zine Events

A zine convention or small press fair will allow you to meet hundreds of other creators at once and can be an incredible opportunity to find new readers for your zine. A personal connection with someone leaves them much more inclined to read your zine. It is overwhelming to attend events like this, so people love to pick up free stuff to look at later. There are dozens of opportunities to sit behind a table with your zine every year in most cities.[6] Sometimes you just have to be creative.

These life-affirming events are great for getting your zine into the hands of stores, distros, libraries, and ultimately, readers. It puts a face to your communication and tends to make people more likely to understand where you are coming from. These events are a great way to find new zines that can really challenge, impress, and encourage you. These are the places where collaborations and friendships are born.

---

6 WeMakeZines.com/events

shawn granton ★ may 2008

touring: when in reno, eat the raw pie!

In 2001, I proclaimed that I would make zines as valid a part of punk rock as the music. I shut down my stagnant record label and made a list of of all of the ways that I could show that zines were fascinating and credible. In 1980, hardcore pioneers Black Flag built the DIY punk movement by creating their own touring network without managers, agencies, record labels, or concert promoters. They toured VFW Halls and created the bones of a punk touring network still in use today. I used that same network for zine touring, organizing five different zinesters to get in a car together for a month and have our Black Flag moment.

Naturally, plenty of people had done this same thing before us. The Kill Zinesters Tour in 1996 was sponsored by Epitaph Records to drive from city to city and set up tables featuring their zines. There was no presentation or reading. It was just an effort to make zines into more of a real-life social network than the asocial variant of writing letters to strangers that you'll probably never met. I envisioned something more structured, more like the punk rock tours that I had done. Then, three months before we hit the road, I heard that five friends from New Orleans were doing their own zine reading tour up to New York City with a scrappy punk aesthetic. I feverishly wrote them a letter, asking for any advice. They said that they argued the whole time. So did Black Flag. In that regard, we were much more successful than we imagined possible and our peers.

I called all of my old resources for booking bands as well as the stores along the route that had sold our zines. Between these and talking to a few friends who had either visited the remaining cities or had a friend there, we had quite a list of venues. I began emailing, calling, and mailing out packages of zines. For two weeks, I spent about eight hours per day organizing the tour. The previous punk tours I had organized wound up with a lot of dead ends and disinterested promoters. Our zine tour, Copy & Destroy, was the opposite. If I could speak to the person in charge of events and had a concise explanation of our performance and subject

always bring a pillow!

matter, they said yes. We did a show at every venue that I talked to, sometimes having more than one event in each city. Most places were downright enthusiastic. Sometimes we sent a care package to the store and it was intercepted by an excited employee who took the zines home to read! In every case, the owner saw this as a testament to the quality of our work. We also tabled at some other zine fests along our way.

We ended up with 28 shows in 26 days, performing in people's houses, coffee shops, art galleries, punk venues, infoshops, rock clubs, bookstores, and libraries. We canceled one show at a coffee shop in Reno, when, upon showing up, we discovered that it was full of cops and decorated with homophobic posters.

We sent out postcards to people who ordered our zines in all of the states we were visiting and mailed posters and flyers to the stores and our friends in those cities. We sent press releases to magazines and newspapers, which resulted in them printing calendar listings and articles that weren't remotely accurate, often with wild speculation and hyperbole.

These newspaper articles drew people that weren't aware of zines or active in young, progressive communities. They still bring up that they were disappointed that our performances didn't include karate chops, photocopying demonstrations, or anarchist proselytizing. Though this allure just drove our mystique home.

Loading up the rental car with five people and the resulting amount of zines, books, and personal possessions was quite cramped. But lacking personal comfort was a pain that we happily shared together, for the most part. A few university shows covered our costs to rent a car and for a month of gas. Like Black Flag, we slept on floors and scrounged food at grocery stores.

Between us we sold nearly one thousand zines on that first tour. We had enough money left at the end of the tour that we argued about how to divide it. That is an important parable if there ever was one. People feel like a part of something when they fail together but are suspicious that they aren't being treated fairly when there is abundant success. Have a plan in advance for best and worst case scenarios.

After that tour I realized that we should diversify the presentation to maintain the audience's attention span so we added film, discussion, a raffle, slide shows, and props. Alternating these mediums is great for keeping people actively engaged.

Years later, I recognize that we should have thought bigger, taking a more guerilla approach and performing on the street or selling out of the trunk of a car. This is where lifelong relationships begin and how audiences are found!

I know it sounds clichéd, but really, publishing your own work is its own reward. Have a blast, and may you use your creative power to achieve whatever success you desire. We wish you success—on your own terms.

appendices / resources

In previous editions we compiled resource lists but for this edition, I wanted to support community zinemakers who have slogged through compiling comprehensive resource lists:

WeMakeZines.com: Huge online social network for zinesters

StolenSharpieRevolution.org: A rad book and resource project that you should support.

Queer Zine Archive Project: Qzap.org

ZineWiki.com: A rad, open-source Zine Encyclopedia

List of **Zine Libraries**: zines.barnard.edu/zine-libraries#ore

Whatcha Mean, What's a Zine?: a collaborative, fun book about zines!

Notes from Underground by Stephen Duncombe, the politics of zines!

$100 & A T-Shirt, my 71-minute feature documentary film about zines.

XerographyDebt.blogspot.com, a friendly place that reviews your zine.

PioneersPress.com, a zine distributor in rural Kansas.

MicrocosmPublishing.com

SUBSCRIBE TO EVERYTHING WE PUBLISH!

Do you love what Microcosm publishes?

Do you want us to publish more great stuff?

Would you like to receive each new title as it's published?

Subscribe as a BFF to our new titles and we'll mail them all to you as they are released!

$10-30/mo, pay what you can afford. Include your t-shirt size and month/date of birthday for a possible surprise! Subscription begins the month after it is purchased.

microcosmpublishing.com/bff

...AND HELP US GROW YOUR SMALL WORLD!